W9-BSF-367

PRODUCING, FINANCING AND DISTRIBUTING FILM

PRODUCING,
FINANCING
AND
DISTRIBUTING FILM

Paul A. Baumgarten

Donald C. Farber

Drama Book Specialists (Publishers)
New York

Copyright © 1973 by Paul A. Baumgarten and Donald C. Farber
First edition

Fifth printing

All rights reserved

DRAMA BOOK SPECIALISTS (PUBLISHERS),
150 West 52nd Street, New York, New York 10019

Library of Congress Catalog Card Number: 72-87054
ISBN: 0-910482-31-4

Library of Congress Cataloging in Publication Data
Baumgarten Paul A.
    Producing, financing, and distributing film.
    1. Moving-picture industry—United States.
I. Farber, Donald C., joint author.   II. Title.
PN1993.4.U6B32   658'.91'791430973   72-87054
ISBN 0-910482-31-4

iv

For Annie and Sue with thanks

ACKNOWLEDGMENT

Although writing a book is an unbelievable amount of work, it is, of course, most satisfying when the book is finished and finally appears in print. With us the writing was doubly difficult since we both have other very time consuming duties, and even arranging work sessions involved complicated negotiations.

The collaboration has been a good one and in addition to thanking each other, special thanks should go to the persons who helped with the large chore of typing the manuscript; Dale Burg, who handled the major share of the typing with assists from Sharon Filus and Diana Russell.

Paul's partner, Stephen H. Gross, spent many Saturdays and numerous evenings reading the manuscript and gave us many valuable comments and suggestions both as to form and substance. Harold Berkowitz read portions of the book and made many contributions. In addition, Sidney Kiwitt read the galleys and gave us the benefit of his many years experience in the motion picture industry. Although we listened carefully to those who had an opportunity to read the manuscript, the book is ours and, obviously, we have to accept full responsibility for what it says. We confess that we did not always agree with each other. Therefore, the book, to some extent, is an amalgam of views which sometimes differ, but we stand behind the finished product.

Ralph Pine, our editor-publisher, was and is most patient, extremely helpful and a good friend, but then Ralph must assume at least part of the responsibility for getting us into this.

We do hope that your use of the book will be as meaningful to you as the writing of it has been to us.

TABLE OF CONTENTS

INTRODUCTION

Everyone knows that film is big business. Some of Hollywood's warhorses have cost as much as $10 or $15 million (or more!) to make; now, films more commonly cost between $1 and $2 million. Occasionally, a sleeper comes in for a half-million dollars or less and manages to make it—which means, of course, that the profit participants and financers make a lot of money.

Although there are fabulous success stories surrounding a few "low budget" films that have grossed tremendous sums, most films usually end up in limited distribution at a loss to the financier. Of course the risk is commensurate with the potential profit, and because of this there will always be people ready, willing, and able to finance and make films.

It may be true that there is no business like show business, but we are still waiting to hear someone say that "there is no business like the motion picture business." The motion picture business is a most complicated and most confusing state of affairs. There are many people in the business who are ready to take advantage of the devoted, unknowing persons who are willing to spend their good time, energy, and effort in making motion pictures. It is a big business that requires the extensive knowledge and constant attention necessary for any big business.

We have been in this business for a long time and have negotiated and written many, many contracts, covering every facet of the film industry. Not a week goes by, however, that we aren't confronted with something new and different in a contract negotiation or contract provision—a different twist, a different angle, a different way of defining something, a different way of getting something. For this reason no book can answer all of your questions. That is an impossible task! We have striven for clarity, in hope of enlightening the reader. You may want to study certain parts of this book; you may even find yourself re-reading certain paragraphs more than once and sometimes more than twice.

A film is a totality. All of the parts that go into the business of putting a film together are interrelated, each component dependent in some measure upon the others. For example, certain terms used in the production-distribution agreement must be related to the terms used in the star's contract. The way in which net profits are defined in the production-distribution agreement can determine whether payment to the star is deferred or based on a percentage of the producer's net profits. It would be nice if one could get an overall view at one glance, but this is not possible.

In negotiating a particular contract, one may give up something to get something in exchange. The usual thing about some of these contracts is that they are written so that you may gain a tremendous advantage in one respect, only to have it more than cancelled out later if you lose a negotiating point on some other item. This will become apparent as you read this book.

Bear in mind, also, that were we to write a book four times as long as this, we would still be unable to set forth all the exceptions that occur every day, exceptions to what is the general, the usual, the not unusual.

There is a limit to how completely one may define the terms of some contracts, which are really by most standards almost indefinable. We have tried to define such terms in great detail, making them as simple as possible.

Attorneys often spend many hours negotiating the meanings of terms such as net receipts and gross receipts, whose final meanings can change as variables are introduced in the course of drawing up a contract. We hope to prepare you to expect such variables. In some instances, the full meaning of some terms cannot be completely comprehended without having a thorough knowledge of the law relating to such terms. Again, there is a limit to how much one can cover in a book. Each chapter of this book contains ten or more specific items, each of which could be detailed subjects of law review articles. We have not avoided defining such terms in a general way, but many terms defy precise definition because many terms may be interpreted in many ways.

For example, some people mistakenly think that *gross receipts, gross profits, net receipts,* and *net profits* are terms having a specific meaning. We try to explain to our clients that these terms mean anything anyone defines them to mean. We are always troubled when a client says, "Wow, did I make a.great deal. I'm getting 35% of thus and so." He talks as if the "35% of thus and so" is a fixed, easily definable amount, whether the "thus and so" is gross profits, gross receipts, net profits, net receipts, gross income, net income, or some other combination of these. The "thus and so" has to be clearly defined before the 35% means anything.

It would be very nice to be able to say that there is an easily definable term for net profits, net receipts, gross profits, and gross receipts, but such is not the case. In writing this book, we had the choice of attempting to define the terms completely or of being very flip in giving them a quick definition. When one considers that contracts that include definitions of these terms often require 30 double-spaced typewritten pages to define any one of them, one must pause before trying to over-condense or over-simplify.

We soon discovered that some of the terms which are so common to those of us working in the business are used infrequently outside of a particular aspect of the film industry. We found that defining some of the terms in simple, non-legal language was somewhat of a problem. For an example, *cross collateralization* and *arm's length transaction* have specific meanings that most people in the business understand. To define them simply is not easy. No single definition of any of these terms will be applicable in all contexts. Also, be cautious of terms like *deferral,* for one must know until when the payment is deferred and what takes precedence over the deferred payment.

We very seriously considered including some typical forms as part of this book; however, we came to the conclusion that this would serve little purpose. A typical budget might add 30 pages to the book; but the budget would be totally useless except to give some indication of what a budget looks like. It could not be used to help you write another budget because each film is so special and individual that its budget must be tailored to fit the particular film.

The same can be said for a typical production-distribution agreement. It would add another 40 or more pages to the book, but you would learn very little about general production-distribution agreements. Hopefully, the discussion of each of the possible terms of a production-distribution agreement—which we have discussed in detail and in depth—will be of more value than a form.

Finally, no book on this subject is a substitute for a production manager and an attorney. Nor can you hope to read this book and expect to learn what one learns from 20 years experience in negotiating contracts. It can, however, help you to understand all of the components that go into the business of putting a film together, financing it, and getting it distributed and exhibited. It will be helpful to you to know what your production manager is doing and what your attorney is doing. It will be helpful to you to know and understand some of the contracts which you may negotiate yourself if you are producing a film. It will be helpful for you to have a knowledge of some of the terminology which is thrown around in the business, which some people think they understand but actually know very little about.

This book was not easy to write; it will not be easy reading, nor will it be easy to understand. But anyone interested in really understanding it can do so by studying it. Anyone willing to spend the time working at it will learn much about contracts involved in producing a film.

Chapter One

ACQUISITION OF A LITERARY PROPERTY

Each motion picture is based on an underlying *property*. The property can and does take many forms. It may be a well-known novel, a play, or an original screenplay; or it may first have taken form as a story outline, or merely a concept. Sometimes a literary property is purchased mainly for the title. In any event, a producer who is about to produce a motion picture must first acquire motion picture rights to the property. From the property everything else flows; the writing is the starting point for the entire motion picture.

If the original property is an artistic failure, it is difficult to see how a motion picture based on it would be financially successful. On the other hand, although unlikely, it is possible that the producer may have a novel idea or some method by which an unsuccessful book, rewritten or treated in a certain manner, could become a very popular and successful motion picture. Nevertheless, the job of the producer is to acquire motion picture rights to a literary property and to develop it to a point at which an investor or a motion picture distributor would be willing to finance its production.

For example, let us examine what happens when a producer becomes interested in a certain book, first published in the United States, on which he wants to base a motion picture. The book, which the producer believes will make a successful motion picture, is usually a published book. Since most producers do not have unlimited funds, they usually attempt to acquire an option to purchase motion picture rights to the book. The motion picture rights to the book may have been retained by the author or acquired by a publisher, and the contract between the author and the publisher should be examined to determine how the rights are divided.

Many producers are able to obtain manuscripts in galley or prepublished form. In this case, the facts are more difficult to ascertain. The usual approach is to contact the author or the author's agent to negotiate the terms of a deal.

If a book is not too well known, it is not unusual for the producer to acquire an option for between six months and two years, for a payment of between $500 and $5,000 or more, depending on the bargaining power of the parties. Some variables are the author's reputation, the number of copies sold, the successful penetration in a particular market, and whether or not the author will write the script. If possible, the right to extend the option for additional periods should also be obtained. Generally, if the option is exercised, whatever is paid for the option applies toward the purchase price of the motion picture rights of the book. If there is more than one option, subsequent option payments are sometimes retained and not credited toward the purchase price.

The first step should be to make sure that you are dealing with the actual owner of the rights. If the author is represented by a reputable agent who claims that the author owns the rights being sought, it is reasonably safe to assume that this is the case. To make certain, it is customary to make a *copyright search* in one of two ways.

The first method is a search of the records in the U.S. Copyright Office in Washington, D.C., to determine whether or not a *copyright registration* of the book has been filed, and if so, who the *copyright proprietor* is. The prudent author usually sees to it that the copyright of the book is registered in his own name. However, on occasion, a publisher may register the copyright of the book in the publisher's name and then reassign the copyright to the author, reserving only those specific publishing rights that the publisher requires. The copyright search will also disclose recorded assignments relating to the work.

The second method is to engage one of several organizations that keep a copyright registration file, press clippings, and other records relating to specific titles. As will be later discussed in detail, this additional information sometimes gives a clue to possible outstanding option agreements, uses of the work for radio or television performances, and other similar titles which might not be revealed in a copyright search.

If the copyright search reveals no copyright registration whatsoever, it does not necessarily mean that the work is in the public domain. It may merely mean that no registration was filed. If the work bears a proper *copyright notice,* it is protected, barring special circumstances, even in the absence of registration. If the work bears a copyright notice, the film rights should be acquired from the party whose name appears on the copyright notice, unless there is clearly documented chain of title indicating some other proprietor. If the work is unpublished the author owns all rights under common law copyright.

If the book has been published outside the U.S., it is even more important to examine the book to see what copyright notice, if any, appears. If the book bears a form of copyright notice required by the Universal Copyright Convention, the book is protected in the U.S. as well as in all countries that are parties to the convention, which include most of the major entertainment markets of the world.

If the work is copyrighted in the U.S. and published simultaneously in the U.S. and Canada—a Berne Union signatory—the work is protected under the Berne Union in all Berne Union countries. This is the reason the title pages of some books state that copies of the book have been simultaneously offered for sale in Canada. Ordinarily, the U.S. book publisher will get an affidavit to that effect from the Canadian distributor.

If one of the principal reasons for acquiring rights to a book is to use a unique or interesting title, it is advisable to have a title

3

search made to determine if there are conflicting titles of books, films, or other properties that might lead to claims of unfair competition. Since titles of books cannot be copyrighted unless the title is extraordinarily long, the only way a title is protected is under the law of unfair competition. It must be shown that the title is associated in the mind of the public with the claimant's work, and that someone else is passing off his work as the claimant's, thus creating confusion. Many financier distributors are signatories to the title registration procedure of the Motion Picture Association of America. That procedure gives the first registrant of a title certain rights which may prohibit another member from dealing with the title even though the laws of unfair competition might otherwise permit that other member to use the title.

Assuming that the rights are in order, the next step is to negotiate for an exclusive option. The producer should obtain an option that will extend for a long enough period to do development work on the property, and to arrange financing and motion picture distribution for the proposed film. For this reason, the option agreement should always provide that as long as the option is in effect, the producer has the right to engage in certain preparatory work with respect to the property—such as the writing of the screenplay, the preparation of budgets, preliminary casting—and to announce that the property is being developed.

The option agreement between the author and the producer typically has annexed to it some form of *literary purchase agreement* that will become effective if the option is exercised. Sometimes in lieu of an option agreement there is an initial outright grant of the rights, subject to reversion to the owner if the full purchase price is not paid. In such case the first installment would be the same as the option price and the principal payment (the purchase price) would be the equivalent of the payment made to exercise the option. Ordinarily, it is wise for the producer to have the author execute the form of the literary purchase agreement along with the option. The option agreement should provide that if the option is exercised, the producer or his assignee may countersign the literary purchase agreement, which then becomes effective. Sometimes the entire agreement is one document with the option and purchase provisions combined. The option price often

4

represents about 5% to 10% of the total purchase price payable if the option is exercised.

There are times when a desired literary property cannot be optioned. If there is unusual film interest in the property, or if the author is an important writer or the property is a best seller, the agent may insist upon an outright sale of the rights to the literary property, rather than accepting a lesser sum of money for an option that may never be exercised. Of course, the longer the property is optioned, the longer the author's agent must let it lie; he should not entertain other deals for the property during an option period.

There is no rule of thumb for determining how much should be paid for the acquisition (not just the option to acquire) of a particular literary property. The price may range anywhere from $500 to $10,000 for a short story, article, or unknown novel, and can be as much as $1 million or more for a well-known best seller. In a later discussion of the form of agreement used to acquire film rights to a literary property, reference will be made to the different and varied types of payments, such as an escalation clause pegged to the number of copies of the book sold in paperback, hard cover, or both. If the book is optioned, the purchase price will ordinarily be higher than if the book is purchased in the first place.

Every literary purchase agreement should include the title, the name of the author, the publisher, the date and place of publication (if previously published), and any copyright registration information. If the work is in manuscript form, it is a good idea to identify it by the number of pages and the date of its completion. If the author has entered into an agreement for the publication of his book, that may also be described. The date for the publication of the book set by the publishers should be referred to also since part of the purchase price may be based upon the anticipation of publication. Of course, if the book is a financial success, it is much easier to finance a motion picture based on it.

The agreement usually states that the purchase price of the book includes rights to the plot, theme, title, characters, prior and future translations, adaptations, and versions. Sometimes the agreement will also provide that any sequels to the book that may

5

be written by the author become the property of the purchaser, and that the purchaser acquires the same rights in the sequels that he acquired in the original property. Quite frequently, the author's agent (with some justification) will take the position that only the rights to one particular book are being sold and the purchaser should acquire no rights to any sequels or characters in the original book. The resolution is frequently the retention of sequel or character rights by the author, but the prohibition of the transfer or utilization of rights similar to those granted to the purchaser for a given number of years. This subject will be discussed later in greater detail.

If the book was originally written in a foreign language, or if the book contains illustrations, and the purchaser is acquiring rights to the illustrations, the purchaser must make sure that the author owns the rights to the illustrations or translation so that the author may assign these rights to the purchaser. If the author does not own such rights, the purchaser must negotiate separately for these rights as well. Since the author may revise the book, may permit its translation into another language, or may write different versions of it, the purchaser must make sure that he acquires the same film rights to the revision, translation, or other versions that he acquires in the property. This ensures against the possibility of the motion picture rights to the book being sold twice in two different versions to two different purchasers.

From the point of view of a producer who is only interested in producing a motion picture, certain rights—other than the rights to make one motion picture—may not seem important. But from the point of view of a financier or a motion picture company, which may desire to turn a motion picture property into a remake, a sequel, or a television special or series, these other rights are very important and may affect the kind of deal that a distribution company or a financier will make with the producer. For this reason, the producer commonly tries to acquire the right to make any number of motion pictures, whether or not produced initially for television or theatrical release.

This would include a remake motion picture or a sequel motion picture. A sequel motion picture utilizes a principal character or characters or plot device of the original picture, but puts them in new situations—such as a different plot. A remake of a picture is

6

usually the same story retold and possibly brought up to date. The literary rights may be utilized in a musical, narrative, or any other kind of motion picture. The motion picture can be exhibited in any form, such as wider or narrower negative width, or self-contained cassettes or cartridges, and distributed in any manner, including theatrical exhibition, non-theatrical exhibition (auditoriums, colleges, clubs), and free or pay television.

The film industry distinguishes in this connection between the rights to make a feature-length motion picture production, which may be released on television, and a television production, which may or may not be released theatrically. Therefore, if both the right to make feature films and television programs or series are acquired, the different categories of rights should be clearly set forth. In addition, excerpts of a film can be used in a featurette for advertising and promotional purposes.

The producer should also acquire the rights to utilize the property for television. The television rights are generally categorized as film, taped, or live television rights. Filmed or taped television rights are the rights to record the program, usually either on videotape or 16mm film. Live television is becoming outdated. since almost every live television program is videotaped for delayed broadcasting in other markets. A filmed television program is intended to be syndicated—that is, repeated a number of times in each market. A live television program, if prerecorded, can only be shown once in each market, unless the contract specifically provides for additional uses. Ordinarily, the producer acquires filmed television rights—that is, the rights to produce and market an individual television program and television series. Live television rights are generally reserved to the author.

The purchaser should attempt to acquire at no additional cost all radio rights—that is, the rights to broadcast the property or excerpts of it by means of radio, either by live actors or by records or transcriptions. The purchaser, at the very least, must acquire the right to advertise and promote the motion picture by means of radio and television. The author may insist that these broadcasts be limited in time, usually to five minutes each, and that the producer receive no financial remuneration with respect to such broadcasts.

The producer will acquire the right to write short synopses or

7

summaries of the property, usually not exceeding 7,500 or 10,000 words each, that are utilized for advertising and promotional purposes.

Even if a literary property has been published, it is sometimes possible for the producer to acquire the rights to publish the script or a novelized version of the script of the picture. This is usually done for promotional purposes in connection with the release of the motion picture. In addition, it may be possible to obtain the right to utilize excerpts of the property in publishing a book about the filming of the motion picture. Ordinarily, the author of the original property would ask to share in any royalty or advance received by the producer for any publication rights.

Usually, the author would not want to write the novelized version of the screenplay, which is frequently merely a routine rewrite of the script, and the author would therefore insist that he not be credited as author. If such publishing rights cannot be acquired from the author because the author reserves them or has previously conveyed them to a publisher, it may be possible to make a tie-in deal with the publisher of the paperback version. This would permit the publisher to utilize the motion picture advertising artwork as part of his publishing promotion. The paperback version containing the artwork would be published near the release date of the motion picture and would become a promotional device for the film, as well as for sales of the book.

Usually, the purchaser of a literary property does not acquire the dramatic stage rights to that property. Such rights are reserved to the author, as will be discussed later.

Generally, the purchaser of motion picture and allied rights to a literary property acquires the exclusive rights to use merchandise or commercial tie-ins connected with the property, or any versions of the property. Additionally, the purchaser acquires the right to utilize the title of the property in connection with the picture, and sometimes, for any of the other rights acquired. For instance, the title could become the title of a musical composition or a television series.

Certain rights in the literary property are reserved to the author. Many author's representatives want the contract to state that all rights not specifically granted the producer are reserved to the author. The representative argues that the producer is acquiring only certain limited rights, that it is up to the producer to spell out the rights he wants, and that if the producer does not identify those rights, they are reserved to the author. On the other hand, the producer's representative argues that he cannot chance that some now unforeseen use may preclude him from doing the very thing for which he has bought the literary property. If broad language is used in the clause that gives the producer the right to any and all uses of the property regardless of when they are devised, it contradicts the clause stating that all rights not specifically granted to the producer are reserved to the author. There might be a question whether or not a new use was, in fact, granted to the producer or reserved to the owner.

A possible solution to this conflict is to provide that all rights analagous to the rights specifically granted to the producer are granted to the producer, and all rights analagous to the rights reserved to the author are, in fact, reserved to him.

The author reserves all publishing rights, except for the rights usually granted to the purchaser to write synopses or fictionalizations, and the possibility that the purchaser may obtain the right to publish the script or to write a novelization of the script for promotional purposes.

It is customary to provide that the author's reserved rights do not relate to anything done by the producer in connection with the literary property. For example, if in writing a screenplay a new character is added by the screenwriter, the author does not acquire any rights to that character.

Usually, the author will reserve so-called "live" television rights and dramatic rights, but there is no logical reason why it is customary for the author to grant television series rights or film television rights to the purchaser, at the same time reserving live television rights for himself; nor is there any logical reason for most motion picture distributors not to insist that the purchaser of movie rights acquire dramatic rights. Supposedly, the theory is that motion picture producers are interested in what goes on film—that is, the motion picture, the filmed television rights, the possibility of taped or recorded radio rights—and that the transitory uses of the property, such as a one-time live television program or a stage play, are not the primary interest of most motion picture producers; nor do they have any expertise in

9

utilizing such rights. Therefore, the author often reserves such rights for disposition to someone who could use them better, although such disposition may be limited by the motion picture sale agreement. In fact, producers and film distributors frequently invest in stage presentations. The coordination of live and filmed presentations of a work is important in insuring that there will be no competition in the exercise of the rights.

The author will agree, however, not to utilize any of his reserved rights to compete with any of the rights granted to the producer for stated periods of time, and the producer may receive a right of first or last refusal. There is a wide variation in the time periods. An author's representative will take the position that a restriction of the use of such rights for a period of three to five years from the date of agreement, or two to three years from the first public exhibition, or possibly the first general release of the purchaser's first motion picture, is more than sufficient.

The use of alternative dates, from agreement and from release, gives the author assurance that on an ascertainable date the restrictive period will end, but the producer is given time from the date to produce and release the picture. The theory is that three years from the first public exhibition takes the picture through theatrical release and into network release on television. The producer argues that this period should be for seven to ten, and five to seven years respectively to protect the picture through theatrical release, into network release, and through television syndication.

The author also customarily reserves the right to write a sequel to the property. Since the author could write one sequel after another and thus force the producer to keep purchasing the sequels, the producer should insist on a long restriction in the time period within which competitive rights can be sold or utilized. This will protect the producer's rights in the first book published.

In addition, the producer should acquire with the original literary property all sequel rights except for full-length published sequel books. In that way, the purchaser can assure himself that the author must at least write a full-length bona fide work to preserve the author's rights, and not force the purchaser to purchase a sequel short story to protect character rights in the original work.

Furthermore, the purchaser should try to get what is called a

10

right of first or *last refusal.* A right of last refusal is the right to match any third party offer, in the event that the author seeks to exercise or sell any of the reserved rights other than the publishing rights. If the offer isn't matched, the rights can be sold to the third party. A right of first refusal obligates the author to offer the rights at a price to the producer. If the offer is rejected, the person making the offer can sell to a third party at the offered price or at a price more favorable to the person making the offer. In either event, the producer has the chance to acquire the rights himself, even if in acquiring them he does so only so that someone else will not use them. To verify that the author has accepted a better deal than the producer's, the agreement should provide for delivery of a copy of the executed third party sale agreement.

It is surprising that the one part of the typical literary purchase agreement that is almost never questioned is the unlimited right of the producer to vary, change, modify, and rearrange the property and characters in any way he wishes. From the producer's point of view, he must have this exclusive right because if the author has any veto in the development or production of the property, there may be an impasse and the producer's money will have been lost. For some reason, with a dramatic production it is different: not a single word can be changed without the author's permission. Probably, the difference is that in making a film, the literary property is translated into another medium, whereas in a dramatic production it is not. Most often the author accepts this point as non-negotiable and resigns himself to the fact that he has no control over the ultimate form of the film. The author, if he is paid enough for the rights, relies on the producer's good faith and reputation, or on the reputation of the screenwriter. The important point is that in any agreement involving rights, how the rights are controlled and who makes the final decision must be made clear.

Most literary purchase agreements contain a clause in which the author waives any rights of so-called *droit moral.* In the United States, the validity of such a clause has been upheld, but in some foreign countries, especially France, the author cannot legally convey to anyone the right to drastically change the author's work. In such countries, any waiver of the *droit moral*, or the moral right of the author, is invalid. If the literary property were purchased from

11

a French national, it is conceivable that the motion picture which materially changed that property could violate a French author's moral right. If the film were released in France, the author could conceivably have a claim. On the other hand, the author's making the claim would constitute a violation of his agreement and would be grounds for a law suit by the producer in America.

The producer acquiring the broad spectrum of rights, as just enumerated, generally makes one of several types of payment. First of all, there is the payment for the film rights in the literary property itself. If the payment is a cash payment, it may be made at the execution of the agreement, or if the author agrees, it may be spread over a period of time. The spreading of the payment may be a tax-saving device to defer the income of the author over a period of years; the most important consideration is the solvency and the financial stability of the producer, for if the producer goes out of business, the author may not get the balance of his money.

There may also be contingent payments based on sales of the book after it has been published. One common formula is the payment to the author of 50 cents per copy of the trade edition sold in the U.S. and Canada for a period of two (or three, four, or five) years after first publication in excess of 30,000, 40,000, or 50,000 copies. The trade edition is the original published version of the book and is usually defined as an edition for which the retail price is not less than a stated sum of money. The producer is usually willing to pay the additional amount if the book in fact sells large quantities, because if it does, it is obviously a huge success and the film rights are all the more valuable. Some producers do not want to pay contingent payments based on the number of books sold after the release of the film on the theory that the film is then selling the book and not vice versa.

In addition, there may be a payment of money based on the paperback sales. For example, the producer may pay the author 2 cents per copy for each paperback sale in excess of one million copies in the U.S. and Canada. The theory is the same here—the more sold copies in circulation, the more the book is known and, theoretically, the more people will go to see the movie.

Sometimes, payments are made for each week the book appears on the *New York Times* best seller list. For example, a payment of $1,000 per week may be made for each week the book rates one

12

through five on the list, and $500 per week for numbers six through ten. Sometimes cash payments are made for each adoption of the book by a well-known book club, such as the Book of the Month Club or the Literary Guild.

These additional payments generally apply only to works by well-known authors, or with unpublished books that seem to have the potential of being best sellers.

If a producer cannot afford to make a substantial initial payment to acquire the motion picture rights to a literary property, he will sometimes give the author a *deferment,* or percentage of net receipts (or gross receipts), of the first motion picture produced, or a payment which will be made upon commencement of principal photography of the movie. The producer may assume that if he is ready to commence principal photography of the photoplay, he will at that time have enough money to make the author's payment. A deferment, as will be discussed later, is a contingent obligation to pay a fixed sum of money from the net receipts of the picture, usually payable immediately prior to the payment of net profits.

It is usual for the producer to give only a percentage of whatever net receipts he receives. As will be discussed later, net receipts are divided a number of ways, and the producer gets only a percentage of all of the net receipts, subject to many different kinds of deductions, depending on various contingencies.

If the purchaser of a literary property is making a payment to the author consisting of a percentage of the producer's net receipts, he must be careful about how the agreement is worded. If the producer assigns the rights acquired in a literary property to an assignee, the assignee's percentage of net receipts and the way this percentage is calculated may differ materially from the net receipts the producer might have received. To avoid this problem, the net receipts can be based on a fixed percentage of 100% (that is, *all* of the net receipts, not merely the producer's share).

In addition, a detailed formula for computing net receipts can be annexed to the agreement as an exhibit. The trouble with this alternative is that every distribution company has its own formula, and that formula may vary from the formula used by the producer. The distribution company might object to some of the provisions in the formula utilized by the producer. Financiers and

13

motion picture distributors may insist that any profit participation payable to third parties must be paid from the producer's share only.

It is generally a matter of industry custom to pay one-third to one-half of the original purchase price for every sequel motion picture photoplay, and one-third of the original purchase price for any remake motion picture photoplay. The reason for the percentage difference is that the first picture may be a springboard to a whole chain of pictures—a springboard triggered by the literary property acquired by the producer. Consequently, a higher payment is justified for a sequel. On the other hand, it may be argued that the author should get more for the remake because the remake is based upon the author's work, and not as much for the sequel, which represents more of the creative effort of the motion picture producer. The percentage payment payable to the author may be based on the basic purchase price or may include any profit participations or escalations.

If the producer acquires television series rights, the author ordinarily will be paid for such rights on a per episode basis. Payments are rarely less than $500 for each episode of the series occupying a one-half hour time slot, $750 for one hour, and $1,000 for one and one-half hours. They are usually not more than $750 for one-half hour, $1,000 for one hour and $1,500 for one and one-half hours. Sometimes, an author will try to negotiate additional payments if a particular episode in the series is shown more than once. Usually the price of the reruns is fixed by dividing 100% of the original payment by the number of reruns. The formula is sometimes expressed as 30-25-20-15 and 10 (30% for the first rerun, 25% for the second, etc.) No payments would have to be made for any reruns after the fifth rerun. If the series is to be a daytime series, payments in a similar amount may be applicable to an entire week's episodes, rather than one episode, since the budgets for a daytime serial are usually relatively low.

Sometimes separate payments are made for a television special. These payments will vary greatly and are simply a matter of negotiation, but are higher than the per episode payments.

The following questions will illustrate the necessity for careful drafting. For instance, is the participation calculated on the first

14

motion picture produced, or on the first motion picture produced for theatrical release? Is a television feature which serves as a pilot for a television series considered a motion picture of a feature-length film made for television release, a television special, or one episode of a series? The payment the author gets may depend on the answers. If it is one episode of a television series, the payment on a per episode basis would be relatively low. If it is considered by itself as a television special, the television special payment, which is usually higher, would be applicable. If a feature-length motion picture photoplay based on the literary property had already been produced, the television special might conceivably be a remake or a sequel motion picture photoplay, and a third type of payment would have to be made. These questions can be avoided by careful drafting.

The warranties that the author is usually required to make in a literary purchase agreement are that he alone owns all the rights to the work that the producer is acquiring, and that the work is original and does not infringe on any rights of any person, firm, or corporation. Sometimes the warranties of originality are made to the best of the author's knowledge, information, or belief, but such a qualification will water down the warranty to the point where it is worthless, unless the producer can prove that the author intentionally infringed on someone's rights.

Sometimes the author will try to limit his liability for breach of warranty to the amount that he is paid for the rights. This is done on the theory that he does not want to be exposed to damages in excess of what he receives. Most producers will take the position that the liability should be unlimited since it is the author and not the producer, who knows and should be responsible for the content and originality of what he has written.

It is usually very difficult for a purchaser to determine whether or not a particular work contains infringing material. Additionally, it may be argued that if the author must only return that which he has received, his potential liability is inadequate to insure the reliability of his warranties, particularly in light of the sums involved in producing and distributing a film.

A compromise would limit the author's liability to a multiple of the amount paid to him or some other similar formula. In reality, the compromise may depend more upon how much the author is being paid. If the author is receiving $1 million (which is rare these days), the issue is less important since it is hardly conceivable that the liability of the author for infringement would exceed this amount.

Usually, if there is a claim against the author, the producer will want to be notified promptly, and be given the right to defend the claim and settle it on terms of his own choosing. The producer would also want the right to withhold payment to the author sufficient to cover the claim and costs to defend such an action. This may seem unjust to the author; he may feel that if there is a claim, he should have the right to defend the claim and consent to any settlement. If the author must indemnify the producer, in effect the claim is being settled with the author's money. He would not, therefore, want the producer to settle a claim for an overly generous amount just to be rid of the claim. On the other hand, from the producer's point of view, any claim against the author can seriously impede the sale to a motion picture financier-distributor and can interfere with the release of the motion picture.

If the claim takes place after the release of a film, the damages are multiplied. If the agreement provides that the author must consent to a settlement, and the author refuses to consent because he thinks he has committed no breach, the whole production of the photoplay may be suspended.

In lieu of the author's withholding consent to a settlement, the producer may permit the author to bond the claim. In such a case, if the author can secure a surety bond, the author would be responsible for the defense of the claim, and the bonding company would make good any loss to the producer. As a practical matter, it is unlikely that an author could secure a bond for any type of serious claim. On the other hand, if the literary property is a published work in print for any length of time, any claims of infringement usually would already have been made. If the author has not received notice of a claim after the book has been in print, providing the book has had a general circulation, then it is unlikely that he will, and he probably does not have to worry too much about claims.

16

The duration of the underlying rights in the literary property may create additional problems for the producer. The present U.S. copyright law only protects the rights to a book for an initial period of 28 years. The author himself can renew the copyright if he is living at the beginning of the 28th year. (Although this point is not really settled, there are some copyright authorities who believe that the author has to live through the entire 28th year before he has the right of copyright renewal.) If the author dies prior to the renewal period, the rights vest successively in the widow and children collectively as a class, the executor of the estate, if there is a will, and the heirs if there is not.

If a book has been in print for several years, a producer should check to see how much time remains in the first period of copyright. If the book is 20 years old, there are only eight years left. If the author dies, it may be difficult (and expensive) to acquire a renewal copyright from the author's widow and/or children, who under the copyright laws would collectively have the right to convey the copyright to a third party, since the renewal copyright is considered a new estate. In such a case, when acquiring motion picture rights from the author, it is a good idea at the same time to acquire an assignment of the renewal copyright from the spouse and from any children over the age of 21 years. To be really prudent, one might prepare a codicil for the author that would direct his executor to convey the renewal copyright if there is no spouse or children. In the event that the spouse and children of the author convey copyright renewal rights, there should be a statement in the literary purchase agreement of the consideration paid; in other words, it should be stipulated that the spouse and children are receiving a proportion of the purchase price paid to the author. If an inadequate consideration is paid to the spouse and the children for the renewal copyright, they may properly claim that the conveyance of the copyright renewal is void.

The producer must also consider the question of the billing the author will be given. The author ordinarily will receive screen credit on all positive prints of the photoplay, either on a separate card or on a card with the screenwriter of the photoplay. Under the Writer's Guild of America Minimum Basic Agreement, if a story credit and a screenplay credit appear on the same card, the screenplay credit must appear first, occupy at least 50% of the card, and be in a size type at least as large as that of the author's credit. Occasionally an author will receive credit in paid advertising promoting the motion picture.

A producer will sometimes try to reduce the purchase price for acquisition of the property by providing the author with prominent billing, both on the screen and in paid advertising. From the point of view of a financier-distributor, the fewer the credits the better; the distributor is trying to sell the picture, and there are only certain names that are meaningful to the public. The distributor wants the right but not the obligation to use the name of the author in advertising.

Generally, distributors are much more concerned about what credits appear in advertising than they are about what credits appear on the screen. The advertising sells the film. Once the patron has paid the price of admission and walked into the theatre, it would appear to make little difference how many credits appear on the screen. The common practice of proliferating screen credits may make it seem as though the credits run through half of the picture. The practice is now developing, subject to Writer's Guild requirements, of putting most of the credits at the end of the picture. If the author wants his credit at the beginning of the film, he had better so specify.

In addition to the literary purchase agreement discussed, there are other related agreements that deserve mention. If the agreement is an option agreement, there also should be a short-form option assignment setting forth the fact that the producer has an exclusive option on the literary property. This form should be recorded in the U.S. Copyright Office. If the agreement is an agreement for the purchase of rights to a literary property, there should also be a short form of the agreement that should be recorded. Both short forms serve merely as notice and by the terms of each, should be subject to the full-length agreement. If the work has been published, the producer should obtain a release from the publisher stating that the publisher has not acquired any rights that the producer is acquiring and granting certain advertising rights. This hardly ever presents a problem.

Chapter Two

THE SCREENPLAY AGREEMENT

After a literary purchase agreement has been executed, it is necessary for the producer to find a screenwriter to write the screenplay. Of course the producer may either purchase a completed screenplay or retain a writer to. develop an original story idea from its inception. In either case, the producer generally acquires all rights including publishing rights (of the screenplay) in the following fashion. There are various stages in the writing of a screenplay and the screenplay agreement should provide for all stages. The customary way of obtaining a finished script is to proceed in steps.

1. The first stage is generally called a *treatment*. This is usually a narrative statement of the plot, a description of the main characters and locations, and sometimes sample lines of dialogue—all of which is approximately 20 to 40 pages in length, and will indicate the direction that the screenwriter would proceed in developing a final script.
2. The usual next stage is the *first-draft screenplay*, which

usually requires 12 to 16 weeks to write and usually runs 120 to 150 pages in length. At this point, the dialogue is written and the scenes and the characters are fully defined. Each camera setup and action sequence is indicated.

3. There is sometimes a revised screenplay written, based on the first draft screenplay and the producer's suggestions, which is usually completed in about four weeks.

4. Finally, there is a script *polish* period, which is completed in anywhere from two to three weeks. The producer may expect a screenwriter to work on a screenplay for approximately four to six consecutive months.

After each draft, there is usually a reading and consultation period between the writer and the producer which takes from two to four weeks. During this period the producer reads the screenplay, consults with the screenwriter, and gives the screenwriter any comments or suggestions he may have.

The contractual relationship between the producer and the screenwriter is governed extensively by the terms of an industry-wide collective bargaining agreement, the Writer's Guild of America Minimum Basic Agreement, if the writer or producer are parties to the agreement. It establishes minimum payments for certain work, forbids writing on speculation, and contains detailed billing credit requirements. This agreement should be referred to for the basic payment schedules, which change each time the agreement is renegotiated. Many writers are not guild members and are not subject to guild rules. This includes foreign writers whose contracts are negotiated and executed outside of the guild jurisdiction and who render services outside of guild jurisdiction.

The Writer's Guild of America Minimum Basic Agreement applies to an employee whose contract is executed within the U.S., regardless of where he performs his services. It also applies to an employee whose services are required by the producer to be performed, and are performed, within the U.S., even though the agreement may have been entered into outside of the U.S. The agreement applies to a writer whose services are loaned to the producer by means of a lending corporation.

Ordinarily, the producer should provide in the agreement for certain cutoff stages in the writing of the screenplay. For instance, the producer may pay the screenwriter for a first draft screenplay, but if he does not approve of the first draft, he should be in a position to terminate the writer's services and not pay for revised scripts. The concept can be phrased by having the screenwriter write a treatment, or a first draft, and giving the producer options to require subsequent drafts. If the treatment is approved, the producer exercises the option and a first draft is written. If the first draft is approved, the producer then exercises his option for a rewrite.

Some experienced screenwriters are in a bargaining position and can insist that they write the entire script, including the first draft screenplay, a revision, and a polish, and can also insist on getting paid whether or not the producer approves the first draft or any subsequent draft of the screenplay. Most often, a final screenplay will not be completed until after the director has been selected and engaged, for the director will have his own ideas about the script and will want to work with the writer during the rewriting. For this reason, the producer will want the agreement to provide for at least one rewrite to be done at a later date, after a director has been selected, subject of course to the writer's availability.

Compensation for screenwriters varies widely depending upon prior screenplays (and their success), awards won, experience, and the budget of the film. The screenplay and literary purchase price together should not exceed 10% of the total budget except in unusual cases. Actually, most screenwriters of feature-length motion picture photoplays receive more than the applicable guild minimum, and some screenwriters have received more than $200,000 for a screenplay. Occasionally, in addition to cash compensation a writer will receive either a deferment or a percentage of gross or net profits (which will be discussed later). The same principles that apply to a deferment and a profit participation with respect to an arrangement for obtaining the literary property or for talent would apply to the screenwriter as well.

Some of the provisions of the typical screenwriter's contract merit further discussion. Ordinarily, the agreement will provide that the screenplay must be of such quality that a feature-length photoplay based on the screenplay can be exhibited in a *Class A* theatre in the U.S.

Although this language is frequently used, it sets only a very

21

general and non-objective standard. A screenwriter should use his best efforts in writing, but generally a producer must pay for a screenplay even if it is not exactly what the producer required. Presumably, if the screenplay is utter gibberish, the producer could refuse to pay for it.

Quite often the producer's agreement will require the writer to work exclusively for the producer while the various drafts of the screenplay are being written. If he pays enough money, the producer will feel that he is entitled to the writer's exclusive efforts, for if the writer is working on two or three projects at the same time, the producer cannot be sure that the writer is giving sufficient attention to the producer's project.

Usually, the delivery date for each draft or revision is spelled out in the contract. The producer may or may not be concerned about compliance with delivery dates. Sometimes a producer is pleased if a writer is late in delivery, if the lateness is attributable to the writer's efforts to write a better script. However, if other commitments have been made, and the photoplay is due to start at a specified time, the writer must deliver by a specific time, and in such event there should be a provision inserted into the agreement that "time is of the essence." In addition, if money has been borrowed to finance production, interest will be running on that money.

Most screenplay agreements provide that the producer may revise the writer's work in progress and make suggestions and comments which the writer is to incorporate into the script. Some writers object to this as a matter of principle and feel that they should be permitted to write an entire script and deliver the final results to the producer. Some producers want to see how the writer is doing on a day-to-day basis and want to work closely with the writer during the writing period. Such a producer believes that if the writer is on the wrong track, it is best to find out about it early rather than wait until the screenplay is delivered. The producer usually prevails on this point.

The method of payment in screenplay agreements varies. For cash compensation payable, sometimes the producer will pay half on execution of the agreement and half on delivery of the screenplay. Sometimes he will pay half when the writer starts working

22

and half when the writer finishes. The agreement may even provide for payment after the writer actually writes and delivers a specified number of pages. Other agreements will provide for payment in weekly installments. If there are a number of drafts, roughly 50% to 60% of the cash compensation should be paid for the first draft, 25% to 30% for the rewrite, and the balance for the polish.

It is important to consider what happens if the writer dies or is disabled during the screenplay writing. How much is half of a screenplay worth to a producer? If the producer has to hire another writer to finish the screenplay, the second writer may very well demand the same price he would have been paid if he were to write the entire screenplay in the first place. Because of this, the payment of the bulk of the cash compensation may be conditioned upon the completion by the writer of the entire screenplay. In fact, many contracts do provide that if the writer does not complete the final screenplay on time, he is obligated to return all money he has received. If the writer properly completes the first draft and becomes incapacitated during the writing of a later draft, it is not unreasonable that he keep what he was paid for the first draft. Deferred or net receipts compensation is sometimes payable in proportion to the work completed and at other times is payable only after the complete performance of services.

The agreement may provide for a contingent payment payable the first day of actual filming of the script. This is a beneficial arrangement for a producer, for if he gets the financing to make the picture, such a payment will be part of his budget; if he cannot get the financing for the picture, he has lost nothing.

On occasion, a writer may be paid in the form of a bonus if he gets sole screenplay credit and possibly a smaller payment if he gets a shared screenplay credit in first or sometimes even in second position. The Writer's Guild Agreement has a complicated formula for determining screen credits, and if necessary, the matter of screen credits may be submitted to the guild for determination. The drawback to this procedure is that the contract may provide that any monetary compensation, though keyed to screen credit, not be disclosed to the guild, and it is obvious that such a contractual provision cannot be enforced.

23

The same problem comes up when a writer is hired to do a first draft screenplay with an option for a rewrite and a polish. If the producer does not exercise the option, the writer may insist upon whatever payments were due for the rewrite and the polish if the producer affords the writer sole screen credit or if no other writer is hired. Otherwise, it would be possible for a producer, if the first draft screenplay was very good, not to exercise the option and to use the first draft screenplay as the final screenplay, or to hire a writer to do a minor polish and thus deprive the original writer of income.

Ordinarily, a writer will be paid round-trip transportation and living expenses ($50 per day, more or less) if he is required to work sufficiently far from his residence so that overnight accommodations are reasonably necessary. Sometimes he will receive a weekly sum instead of a per diem for his living expenses. The amount is negotiable. The more established writers also require an office and a secretary at producer's expense while they are rendering service to a producer.

In addition to the fixed compensation, the producer is required to make certain additional payments for union fringe benefits, the amount of which depends on the base compensation paid. The writer also receives residual payments for television exhibition of a motion picture based on television gross receipts.

Under the usual screen writer's agreement, the producer acquires all rights to the screenplay from the writer as an employee for hire and the screenwriter retains no rights at all. However, if the screenwriter writes an original script, he may be entitled to what is called *separation of rights* under the Writer's Guild of America Minimum Basic Agreement presently in effect. The author of a literary property would retain certain rights.

1. The publication rights in the script belong exclusively to the writer, but the writer cannot exercise the publication rights prior to three years from the date of the employment contract, or six months following the general release of the picture, whichever is earlier. The producer does have the synopses and fictionalization rights. If the producer decides to publish a paperback novelization of the script for the

24

purposes of publicizing the picture, he can do so, providing the publication does not take place earlier than six months prior to the initial scheduled release date of the film and the writer is given the first option to write the novelization. If the writer does not want to write the novelization, the writer receives a third of the sum paid to the person who does write it.

2. If the producer does not utilize the dramatic or stage rights at any time prior to two years following the general release of the motion picture, or if the producer does not commence principal photography of the motion picture within five years plus up to six months for *force majeur* postponements, he loses the dramatic rights and they belong to the writer. If the producer exercises the dramatic rights, he pays the writer sums equal to 50% of the minimum amounts payable to an author under the terms of the Dramatists Guild Inc. Minimum Basic Production Contract, which is the contract applicable to Broadway and other first class stage productions.

3. If the producer makes a sequel theatrical motion picture, the writer gets 25% of the fixed compensation paid the writer for his first script. If the screenplay contains a character used as the basis for a television series, the writer receives payments in accordance with the Writer's Guild of America Theatrical and Television Film Basic Agreement. Of course, a writer of an original script could negotiate for rights as if the script were a published work.

If the screenwriter bases his screenplay on a story outline furnished by the producer, the producer may be able to contend that the screenwriter is not entitled to separation of rights since the screenplay would then not be original.

In England, screenwriters are not usually considered employees and work as independent contractors. One difference is that in this country it is customary for a producer to deduct withholding taxes and social security and make other payments as would be made to any employee. More important is the fact that the producer becomes the author of a work for hire and thus automatically is entitled to the U.S. copyright renewal rights, whether or not the writer survives his 28th year of the original period of copyright. In England this is not the case and the author, as an independent contractor, conveys all rights to the producer. The conveyance also includes the U.S. copyright but there is a possibility that if the writer dies, the producer will not own the U.S. renewal of the copyright. In some countries, such as France and Italy, there does not seem to be any set pattern and some screenplay writers reserve to themselves certain rights, such as publishing and dramatic rights.

As previously discussed, there is also the problem of *droit moral* with a foreign screenwriter if the material is changed or altered without his consent.

Some producers may request a screenwriter to work with a collaborator in writing the script. As long as the initial writer's compensation is unaffected, the only problem concerns position of credit since both writers do the same work. If one is disabled, presumably the other will continue. Of course, each writer would receive guild minimum.

Chapter Three

THE AGENT

After the producer has acquired film rights in a literary property and has had a screenplay written, he is then in a position to interest a motion picture distributor or financier in the project. There are of course exceptions to this rule, for producers have successfully approached film distributors with just the literary property and no screenplay. Sometimes a producer will come to a distributor and suggest a property which he believes the distributor ought to acquire for the producer to produce, and the producer gets a job without risking any money at all. The usual difficulty in producing a film is that the producer needs a certain minimal amount of money to develop a project to the point where someone is interested in it, and if no one becomes interested, the producer loses his investment.

It is axiomatic that the more elements a producer can wrap up in a package before going to a distributor or financier, the more definite and concrete the project will be, and the less risk it will entail. If the producer has, in addition to a literary property and a script, a fairly detailed production budget, a proposed shooting

27

schedule, a known director who is willing to direct the picture, and possibly even a principal member of the cast, for all practical purposes the picture is ready to be made, and he will more easily arrange an immediate financing deal.

A successful producer should combine creative ability, salesmanship, and production expertise. He must appreciate the commercial potential of the property he wants to make into a motion picture and assemble the creative elements such as writer, director, and cast. He must then sell the package to a financier or a motion picture distributor.

For a number of reasons, at the time the producer is ready to make a presentation to a major motion picture company, one of the smaller independents, or even to a private group of investors, it may be wise to have a good agent. There are a number of talent agencies that specialize in motion picture production. These agencies have easy access to the offices of the film executives who have the power to decide which photoplays will be produced and which will not. An agent can also make worthwhile suggestions for creative elements. Some agents themselves have substantial creative ability and will advise a producer on how a literary property or a screenplay should be altered to make it better, and how to attractively present the project.

The agent usually charges a flat 10% of all compensation the producer receives. The 10% is not computed on the producer's reimbursement for living expenses, but on the producer's fee, his percentage of receipts, and any other income he derives from the picture. The typical agency agreement entitles the agent to 10% of everything the producer receives in the entertainment field for a stipulated period. Of course the agent would be entitled to a fee on a deal which is made during the stipulated period, even if the deal continues after the stipulated period, as well as a deal which may have been negotiated during the stipulated period and is renewed after that period.

In addition, if a producer makes a film following the termination of an agency contract, the receipts of which are *cross collateralized* with a film made during the agency representation, the agent's commissions are payable regardless of any cross collateralization so that the producer may owe a commission on money

28

not received. Cross collateralization occurs in a mutli-picture deal when the profits from a successful movie are used to reimburse the financier for losses for a not-too-successful movie by the same producer. In some cases, agents have been known to reduce their 10% fee to a smaller percentage and the basis for computation of the commission can be negotiated, depending upon the bargaining power of the producer.

A difficulty with some agencies is that, in their roles as packagers, they represent three or four sides of the same deal and are presented with conflicts of interest. For instance, if they are the agent for the director, the principal artist, and the producer, each may wonder whether the agency is favoring any one of them as against the others, in connection with compensation, credit, and ultimate control of the project. But one should also bear in mind that without this multiple representation, the picture might not be produced. The conflict of interest must be weighed against the benefits the agent can provide in negotiating the deal for the producer and getting the producer entree to sources of financing or to a motion picture distributor.

The agent will also act as a buffer between the producer and the distributor or the financiers. The agent may appear to be the bad guy to protect the producer. If the producer wants something outrageous, he may tell the agent, who then tells the financier or distributor, and if the financier-distributor complains too loudly, the agent will say it was really his own idea and not the producer's. The good guy-bad guy game is a standard negotiating ploy in the film business and the only amazing thing about it is that so many people take it seriously. What it really amounts to is a face-saving device for both the distributor and the producer; each can blame the agent for whatever goes wrong. The agent takes the blame, becomes the butt of jokes—and earns 10% of everything.

29

Chapter Four

PRODUCTION-DISTRIBUTION AGREEMENT: GROSS AND NET RECEIPTS

In discussing the form of production-distribution agreement customarily entered into between the producer and the distributor financing the film, or in discussing any other arrangements whereby the receipts of a film are allocated in some fashion between the producer, financier, and distributor, an understanding must be had of what constitutes the distributor's *gross receipts* from a film and how a distributor's gross receipts are distinguished from the gross receipts of a producer. Generally speaking, a distributor's gross receipts is what a distributor of the film is paid by exhibitors such as theatres and television stations for the right to exhibit the film in theatres, on television, non-theatrically, and in other media. Note the distinction between a distributor's gross receipts and a producer's gross receipts. The producer's gross receipts would be those sums received by a producer from a distributor or distributors of a film.

The distributor's gross receipts in addition to the moneys that a distributor of the photoplay receives from all sources, including exhibition of the picture by theatres, television, and non-theatrical licenses, usually includes receipts from the use of the ancillary rights in the picture resulting from the use of the film, as will be discussed. In considering this definition of gross receipts, there is some variation among the practices of distribution companies depending upon the geographical territory in which they themselves distribute.

In the case of a major motion picture company which itself distributes pictures in the major territories of the world, gross receipts would be the aggregate amount received by each local branch or subsidiary of the distributor.

In the type of distribution pattern engaged in by most of the major studios, there are some small territories in which the majors do not themselves distribute films, and in which distribution is carried on by subdistributors under license from the distributor. The subdistributor, from its gross receipts from its territory, generally has the right to retain its own distribution fee and recoup its own expenses. In other cases, the distribution company distributes in only a few major territories, and primarily through subdistributors elsewhere. Sometimes the subdistributor's total receipts are deemed gross receipts for purposes of accounting to the producer but only if the subdistributor remits the distributors's share to the distributor. If the subdistributor does not remit the distributor's share for any reason, the distributor does not treat the subdistributors receipts as gross receipts for purposes for accounting to the producer.

For instance, if a distributor sublicenses the motion picture to a subdistributor on the basis that the subdistributor first retains its distribution fees and expenses and remits the balance to the distributor. And if the subdistributor collects $100, has fees of $40, and incurs expenses of $60; there is nothing to remit to the distributor, and the distributor does not report the gross receipts of $100 to the producer. If the subdistributor collects $200, has fees of $80, and expenses of $60, and thereby owes the distributor $60, but fails to remit any money to the distributor; then the distributor has received nothing and ordinarily reports nothing to the producer, even though gross receipts were earned on which a remittance was due. This may be a puzzling result, but a distributor does not wish to be a guarantor of collections.

Obviously, if a person is receiving a percentage of gross receipts from a distributor, one very basic question is whether a distributor will be distributing all over the world. If so, or if subdistribution will occur in only a few minor territories, gross receipts will be computed on the basis of the distributor's receipts. If, however, the film is being distributed through subdistributors, either the distributor will guarantee collection from the subdistributors—in which event the subdistributor's gross will be the distributor's gross—or the distributor will report only the receipts actually paid to the distributor by the subdistributor as gross receipts, in which event only those receipts will be treated as gross receipts. From the participant's viewpoint, his decision on the extent of his participation (whether, for example, 5% or 10%) for which he will bargain will depend upon what the distributor will deem "gross receipts" for the purposes of reporting to the participant. A distributor in lieu of providing that only receipts actually paid to it by a subdistributor are gross receipts, may agree that although it will consider a subdistributor's gross receipts as its gross receipts, it will never be required to pay out to the participants more than it collects from a subdistributor. In other words, assuming a participant is to receive 10% of the distributor's gross receipts, if a subdistributor receives $100 from an exhibitor, has fees of $30 and expenses of $100, the subdistributor does not owe the distributor any money. The distributor shows $100 as gross receipts in its reports to the participants but since it received nothing from its licensees, it does not at that point have to pay $10 to the participants. If, however, the subdistributor earns another $300, has fees of $90 and expenses of $150 and remits $60, then the cumulative figures indicate that the subdistributor's gross is $400, and the distributor has received $60. The participant is then entitled to his $40, because the distributor received $60, which is a larger sum than the distributor was required to pay the participant. If the subdistributor's expenses had been $200 instead of $150, so that only $10, instead of $60, had been remitted to the distributor, the participant would receive only $10, instead of 10% of $400 or $40, since the distributor only received $10.

Distributor's gross receipts from a film also include television income and non-theatrical income. They also include income from

33

new uses such as cassettes. For any new use in which the distributor may not actually distribute, the same question arises. Should the gross receipts be based upon what the distributor receives from subdistributors or licensees if the distributor is sublicensing the rights, or what the licensee receives from the disposition of such rights?

In some cases, a picture is licensed to a territory on an "outright" basis; in other words, the distributing company will receive a flat sum from the subdistributor in the territory, and whatever the subdistributor earns from the distribution of the film in the territory in connection with the rights licensed, the subdistributor keeps. This form of distribution is common in the minor territories, or in territories where it is difficult to remit monies. Ordinarily gross receipts are deemed to be the flat sum or sale price received by the distributor. For this reason, most producers provide that there cannot be any outright sales made in major territories.

In the U.S., as a result of the Department of Justice's "Paramount Consent Decree," motion picture distribution companies which are parties to the decree are not allowed to own theatres. However, some companies have been and are leasing theatres on a "four-wall" deal in which the theatre receives rent and the distributor tells the theatre owner which pictures to book and on what terms and keeps all revenue derived from the exhibition. What then are gross receipts? To prevent a participant from claiming that all sums received by the theatre as box office receipts are gross receipts, the distributor should provide that it has the right to make an arm's length deal with the theatre for the picture, in which event only that portion of rentals paid by the theatre to the distributor would be distributor's gross receipts. In the alternative, a distributor can provide that all box office receipts less the cost of running the theatre are the distributor's gross receipts.

Paradoxically, there are some theatre chains and television networks that have started motion picture production and distribution enterprises. Some of the major distribution companies own their own theatres in foreign countries. For the producer, this is both an advantage and a disadvantage. On the one hand, the motion picture distributor owning the theatres has an assured

34

outlet for its product, and if such theatres are well located and operated, the distributor's pictures will be favored over some third party's. On the other hand, the distributor can make self-serving agreements with its own theatres at the producer's expense. The distributor could enter into an exhibition agreement with its theatre providing that an artificially low percentage of the theatre's revenues would be paid to the distributor. The distributor will then only receive a portion of the net receipts from that theatre's distribution of the photoplay on which it must account, but the distributor will retain 100% of the profits of its wholly-owned theatre operation.

Some production-distribution agreements will provide that any agreements entered into by a distributor with a theatre owned by the distributor must be made in good faith. To resolve any question of what is or is not good faith, one very large distributor annexes to its production-distribution agreement an exhibit indicating the terms and conditions pursuant to which it will license films to its own theatres overseas. Although the producer may object to the contents of the exhibit, the distributor's position is very simply that if the producer does not like the terms of the exhibit, the distributor will not exhibit the picture in its theatres. Because of the size and power of the distributor, this may silence all protest.

Distributor's gross receipts include other income. If there is a sound-track album or a single record issued from a sound-track album, income ordinarily received by the distribution company from the sale of such records becomes part of distributor's gross receipts. Ordinarily, the sound-track album will not be a big-selling record unless the motion picture itself is successful and, in many respects, a motion picture distributor may regard the sound-track album as an advertising tool on the theory that each time someone looks at the cover of the album, he is reminded of the picture. The income received is based upon a fixed percentage of the retail selling price of (usually) 90% of the number of records manufactured and sold by the record company, less certain deductions. Generally, the best percentage a motion picture distributor can hope to receive from a record company is a percentage of between 7½% and 10%, of 90% of all records manufactured, sold, and paid

35

for, based on the retail selling price. From this sum any percentage to artists must be paid. The 90% was traditionally based on returns for breakage and now has become something of an industry custom, even though there is no royalty paid for returns even if returned for breakage. From the royalty payment, the motion picture distributor is expected to pay, in addition to the recording artist, any costs incurred by the record company to make the album, such as rerun fees or studio recording costs. Rerun fees are fees payable to the musicians if a score recorded for one medium (motion pictures) is used for another (records).

It should be noted that today, the musical score for a motion picture is usually recorded twice, once for the motion picture and again for the sound-track album. Generally, the quality of sound required to record a motion picture effectively is different from the sound required for a sound-track album. In addition, usually a larger number of musicians are used for the studio recording than for the album. If the studio recording were used as part of the album, a rerun fee to the American Federation of Musicians for each musician used for the studio recording would have to be paid, and this fee would probably be larger than the cost of rerecording the music for the album.

The concept of including money that a distributor receives from sales of sound-track albums as part of the motion picture's gross receipts is warranted if the distributor licenses the sound-track album rights to an independent record company in an *arm's length transaction* (a transaction negotiated in good faith by adversaries to obtain the best terms possible). However, most major motion picture companies have their own record companies and try to preserve the sound-track album rights for their own companies. If the score is particularly marketable, or if the distributor thinks that the picture is going to be a commercial success, the album is important. In any event, the picture company usually believes that it can better control the distribution and promotion of the album through its own record company because the latter will do a better job of coordinating promotion of the album with the picture. Besides, the film company may give the record company more money to promote the album than the album might otherwise warrant, just to help promote the film. Usually, the distributor will bargain for the album rights in the production-distribution agreement and the production-distribution agreement will specify the percentage of the album retail selling price which will be paid into gross receipts.

The distributor's royalty from the album may be a percentage of the wholesale selling price of the record rather than the retail price. The wholesale selling price is generally about half the retail selling price, so 5% of the retail selling price would be approximately 10% of the wholesale selling price.

Music publishing rights are also quite important to the film distributor-financier. Most motion picture distribution companies (many also have publishing company subsidiaries) fight long and hard for the music publishing rights and will not cede ownership of those rights. At the least, the producer will expect that a stated percentage of the publisher's share of income derived from music publishing be included as part of the film's gross receipts. The percentage is usually a hotly debated item. Many contracts provide that between 10% and 25% of the publisher's share of income be considered part of the gross receipts. The exact figure is generally negotiable.

There is a certain type of music publishing income which relates more directly to the success of the motion picture. This is theatrical performing income from certain foreign countries. Movie houses in the U.S. do not pay performing fees to performing rights societies for the right to perform the music in a film, but such fees are paid by the producer of the film to the publishers of the music. All composers of film music convey the theatrical performing rights to the producer as part of the grant of rights, and the fee to the composer includes payment for such rights for the U.S. If the music was not written specifically for the photoplay, the license acquired by the producer from the publisher of the music will include a grant of the U.S. theatrical performing license.

In foreign countries, such as England, France, and Italy, however, performing rights societies license theatrical performances directly, and the movie houses pay a percentage of box office receipts to the societies. The percentage varies, but is generally somewhere around 1%. These performing rights cannot be assigned by the songwriter since they automatically vest in the performing rights society. The more the picture grosses in such countries, the

37

larger are the performing fees. The publishing of this music has little or nothing to do with the collection of the performing fees, so long as there is a foreign publisher and token promotion.

Ordinarily, the foreign publisher in the territory will charge only a small collection fee if it collects these royalties, or the royalties can be remitted directly from the foreign performing rights society to either ASCAP or BMI, depending on the publisher's affiliation. Therefore, the producer has a case for arguing that a larger percentage of this type of income be deemed gross receipts since the promotional function of a publisher is virtually nil.

By the same token, the record distributor of the sound-track income ordinarily pays a royalty to the publisher of between 18 cents and 24 cents per album, of which one-half is paid to the writer as writer's royalties. If the success of the album depends in large part upon the success of the motion picture, the producer has a reasonable argument for claiming that a larger percentage of these royalties be deemed gross receipts.

Actually, there is no reason for a distributor to have publishing rights, except if the distributor has advanced all or substantially all of the money necessary to produce the picture; the distributor would like such an edge. If a hit song should develop from the picture, that edge would be quite substantial and combined music publishing and sound-track income could come to many hundreds of thousands of dollars.

Another contributing source of the distributor's gross receipts consists of income derived from *ancillary rights*. Ancillary rights include whatever rights the producer has acquired from the author of the original literary property to produce a remake, a sequel photoplay, or a dramatic stage play.

In some cases the picture serves as a vehicle for a television series, and the ancillary rights could then become quite valuable. There is no set pattern for the disposition of these rights. Ordinarily the distributor obtains control of the use of these rights from the producer. If so, the production-distribution agreement provides that some portion of the distributor's receipts from the exercise of such rights become part of the distributor's gross receipts.

Sometimes the distributor will only restrict use of the rights to

38

make sure they will not be exercised in competition with the movie. He will not want the producer or any one else to produce a remake, a sequel, or a television series that would interfere with the revenue generated by the first picture.

The distributor's position on the percentage of his receipts for ancillary rights which should be considered part of gross receipts is that if it is producing a television series, or financing a remake or a sequel photoplay, it is taking an additional financial risk, and only a portion of the net receipts from such TV, remake, or sequel received by the distributor should become part of the gross receipts of the original movie. The argument has less effect in connection with the sale of such rights by the distributor to a third party.

If the producer has substantial bargaining power, he may want to retain the right to produce a remake or a sequel photoplay or to involve himself in the television series under a financing and distribution agreement with the distributor. Whether or not he ends up with this right is solely a matter of bargaining power and may in some measure depend upon his expertise in the particular field.

The dispute is sometimes resolved by stating that the ancillary rights are frozen and neither party can exercise them without the other. In other cases, there will be provision for a buy-sell formula. If an ancillary right is desired, the distributor will set a price, and the producer either buys the ancillary right at that price, in which case the producer can exercise rights free of any obligation to the distributor, or sells the ancillary right to the distributor. In either case, the price becomes gross receipts, usually without a distribution fee for the distributor.

From the distributor's point of view, if all or most of the cost of production of the picture is unrecouped, the distributor can simply buy the rights at the unrecouped amount. In such a case, the producer would then retain no financial interest whatsoever in ancillary rights, and of course the producer would not receive any net receipts from the picture. However, if the picture has almost recouped its production cost, there would be more of an arm's length relationship in connection with the disposition of the rights.

Distributor's gross receipts also include merchandising rights. *Merchandising rights* are the rights to utilize rights in the title, featured characters, or props used in the film. Revenue can be derived from dolls, games, etc. Generally, all income received by the distributor from the exercise of merchandising rights becomes part of the gross receipts. Again, depending on the picture, these rights may be extremely valuable. A famous producer of children's movies, for instance, has used these rights for many years with great success.

A *distribution fee* is the distributor's charge or fee for undertaking or effecting distribution of the photoplay. The distribution fee is supposed to cover the sales effort of the distributor, the costs of operating the sales exchanges, sales personnel, and general overhead attributable to the sales effort. If a photoplay grossed enough merely to cover distribution expenses and to allow the distributor to recoup the cost of production expenses, the distributor would soon go out of business. A material portion of the distributor's profit is included in the distribution fees charged to each picture by the distributor. The range of distribution fees varies from approximately 30% to 35% of the gross receipts received from distribution or exhibition in the U.S. and Canada, to approximately 30% to 40% of the gross receipts from distribution in the United Kingdom, and approximately 35% to 45% in other foreign countries.

Actually, it has been said that a distribution fee of approximately 20% would cover the costs of the sales effort in that the cost of sales for a year is about equal to a 20% distribution fee on all pictures of a company distributed in a year. But this margin is insufficient to pay general administrative overhead and the costs of projects which are never made into films for one reason or another. Thus, a distributor will lose money unless at least one or two pictures a year can earn substantial net receipts.

Note that the distribution fee is usually based on a percentage of gross receipts prior to any deductions. Most major distributors invariably follow this pattern in the production-distribution agreements. For films financed by producers without the majors, a distribution fee may be charged on some other basis after certain deductions from gross receipts. In the case of a so-called outright sale, the distributor licenses a picture for an entire territory of a country for a flat sum and the distribution fee is somewhere between 10% and 20% of the gross amount received for its outright license. The fee is less because once the distributor makes the sale, delivers the film material, and gets paid, there is nothing further for the distributor to do, and the lower fee represents the reduced continuing selling effort required.

Ordinarily, the distribution fees for television distribution are the same as those charged for theatrical distribution. Sometimes, instead of charging the theatrical distribution fee, a distributor will fix the U.S. television distribution fee as 25% or 30% of the network license fee. It is not clear what distribution fees will be charged for new uses, such as cassettes. Occasionally, contracts are drafted so that the new uses will be charged the same distribution fees as the old ones. This may or may not work out well for the distributor, but at least it provides some solution to the problem of what fee to charge if there is a new use.

If no fee is specified in the distribution agreement, there could be litigation. Ordinarily, a distributor will not charge a fee based on receipts for the ancillary rights or the music or record rights. However, sometimes a nominal 10% distribution fee of such gross receipts is charged. We believe that such fees are a negotiable item, and distributors will sometimes waive them. Again, it depends on the respective bargaining position of the parties. The producer may argue that the distributor is getting a substantial edge in the music publishing and record rights, and should not charge a fee in addition. The distributor will argue that he has some work to do in collecting the money and is thus entitled to a fee. Rarely will such fee be higher than 10%.

The distribution fees charged in most cases represent the total fee of the distributor and the subdistributor. Some companies charge a slightly higher distribution fee when they themselves do not distribute but use a subdistributor. Some companies using a subdistributor provide that the distributor's and the subdistributor's fee cannot exceed a certain amount. Assume the distributor is limited to a 10% fee, and the subdistributor's fee and the distributor's fee together cannot exceed 45% of the subdistributor's gross receipts; consequently, if the subdistributor charges

35%, the distributor could still charge 10%, making a total of 45%. If the subdistributor charges 40%, the distributor would be limited to a 5% fee. If the subdistributor charges 30% the distributor would charge 10%, making a total of 40%.

Most distribution expenses are in the cost of prints and in the cost of advertising. Much of this advertising may be *cooperative advertising*, in which the distributor and the theatrical exhibitor share a proportion of the cost of ads to promote the picture. The proportion is a matter of negotiation but the advertising is usually shared in the same proportion that the exhibitor and distributor share in the box office receipts. It is difficult to determine what percentage of distributor's gross cooperative advertising represents. If a film is very successful, the cooperative advertising costs for the first weeks will be relatively high but the cost for later weeks will be substantially less since the film is already launched and people only want to know where the picture is playing and when. On the other hand, if the film is a failure, the cooperative advertising costs must still be paid but the distributor's gross receipts may be less than the cost of the cooperative advertising. Many producers attempt to limit the amount the distributor can spend for prints and advertising on a picture. It is paradoxical that some producers take the other tack, and want to make sure that the distributor spends at least a minimum amount on prints and advertising.

When the producer insists on an upper limit which may be spent, it is because he is afraid that the distributor may be buying receipts with its advertising. For example, if the distributor's fee is 30% of the gross receipts and if the distributor spends 98 cents of that on advertising, then the picture must gross $1.40 to pay for each expenditure of 98 cents in advertising. It is unfortunate that occasionally a producer will get a statement from a distributor indicating that the picture is more in the red on a later statement than it was on an earlier one. What can happen, of course, is that a picture can be reissued or released in a particular locale and the distributor may spend money for prints and advertising to try and promote bookings without any success. As another example, there is abnormally heavy advertising in connection with the launching of a picture in a first-run theatre in New York or Los Angeles. If the print and advertising cost is not recouped, the producer may

42

* gross of $1.40 x .30 distributors fee (= .42)+ .98 in expenses = $1.40 (i.e. nothing for producer) [take distr. fee 1ST and add expenses to it before see what's left for producer]

(see pg. 45)

be further in the hole than he was before the picture was first released. Is the distributor being improvident, or doing his best to promote the picture? It depends on whom you ask.

The producers who attempt to fix a minimum which must be spent on prints and advertising want to make sure that the distributor gives the picture some sort of publicity and expends at least a certain amount of money in promoting it. The financier-distributor's answer to this request is very simple. The distributor, having financed the picture, has a stake in it and an investment at risk. Ordinarily, the distributors financing a production refuse to allow producers to put any minimum or maximum limits on the amount to be spent for prints and advertising, and, as a matter of fact, many production-distribution agreements go on at great length to ensure that the distributor can sell the picture any way it wants. The contracts usually give the distributor the broadest possible latitude in distributing the picture. Minimums and maximums are more customary when a distributor takes on a completed film for distribution without an advance payment or financing.

Even if the distributor acts in bad faith, or in the case of malfeasance, it is very difficult for the producer to provide contractually that the distributor should or should not have done something. About the most a producer can hope to obtain in the usual production-distribution agreement is some good faith clause to the effect that the distributor will act in good faith. Whether this language actually means anything is debatable. We doubt that any distributors would admit that they were acting in bad faith in the distribution of a movie. A producer can ask for a *best efforts* clause, but about the most he will receive is a clause to the effect that the distributor will agree to distribute the picture in accordance with reasonable business judgment or some other vague standard. If the producer is putting up part or all of the money to make the picture, and the distributor is merely distributing it, the producer is in a better position to insist upon controlling prints and advertising expenditures. Unless the distributor is making an advance or a minimum guarantee, the only financial stake it has in the picture is its investment in prints and advertising.

The cost of prints, as part of the distribution expenses, is considered to be the cost and expenses of all the preprint and print materials utilized in connection with the distribution of the picture, as opposed to the basic negative material from which 35mm release prints (the prints usually used in the theatres) and 16mm release prints (used for television and non-theatrical exhibitions) are manufactured. Those materials are considered part of the cost of production of the photoplay, and thus not part of "distribution expenses." However, certain additional negative materials may be required for release of the picture overseas, or in dubbed or subtitled versions, and these materials are considered distribution expenses.

Generally, the cost of manufacturing trailers is considered a distribution expense, but distributors usually take a right of election. If trailer income becomes part of gross receipts, trailer costs are a distribution expense; if trailer income is not considered part of gross receipts, the costs of the trailer are not a distribution expense. The distributor will usually try to be in a position to make an election in each particular territory. In some territories, trailers are generally distributed at a loss, so it is better for the distribution company to consider trailer income part of the gross receipts, since the distribution fee and expenses on those receipts will result in a deficit. To the extent that it is profitable to distribute trailers, it is of course better for the distribution company to keep the trailer income out of gross receipts and to absorb the expense of the trailers, thus retaining a profit.

Advertising expenses (other than cooperative advertising) include press books, artwork, and other costs of advertising and promoting the picture, including publicity costs. Some distribution companies will include as part of the advertising expenses an overhead charge based on a percentage of all advertising expenditures on a picture for the company's advertising department. Distributors take the position that if the distribution company did not have an advertising department, these specific costs would be incurred by an independent advertising company, and would justifiably be a charge to the picture as advertising expense. The counter argument is that the distribution company for its fee should in any event cover all overhead charges.

Ordinarily, all turnover or remittance taxes of any kind (the tax

44

on the transfer of money from one country to another) are considered to be distribution expenses, as are any taxes or fees imposed upon the prints or negatives or other personal property.

Other usual distribution charges include the cost of checking and verifying box office attendance and receipts, the cost of errors and omissions insurance (covering claims for infringement, libel, etc.), losses incurred as a result of quota requirements, and industry assessments such as dues to the Motion Picture Association of America. If the dues do not relate specifically to the picture, they are usually prorated over all of the pictures of the particular distribution company for the year.

In arriving at net profits or net receipts which will be shared by the producer and distributor in some manner, the distribution fee is first deducted from gross receipts and then the distributor's distribution expenses are deducted. After those deductions, the distributor-financier will recoup the cost of the production of the photoplay with interest. The cost of production of the photoplay is the actual cost of making the picture. If the distributor is taking an overhead charge, then the overhead charge is assessed on each item of production cost. In other words, if the distributor is advancing the producer $100, and is entitled to an overhead charge of 10%, then, although the producer would get $100, he is charged for $110, which the distributor would recoup.

Most usually, the distributor recoups the cost of the production with interest, and the interest is ordinarily at least 1¼% over the rate of interest charged the particular distributor by the distributor's bank. The 1¼% override is justified by the distributor on the grounds that the distributor, in order to get a line of credit, will ordinarily have to keep money on deposit on which the bank does not pay interest. This deposit is called a *compensating balance*. It can run 20% to 25% of the total line of credit, and therefore, if the interest rate is 6¼%, 20% of that charge is 1¼%, which reflects the cost of the compensating balance. Note that the interest is always recouped before the cost of production items are recouped. This is a standard loan financing procedure, and of course increases the interest charged. Interest is charged on overhead and some producers provide that overhead not be charged on interest!

45

After recoupment of the cost of production, deferments are usually paid over. A deferment is a contingent but fixed sum of money payable only from gross receipts prior to the payment of net profits. As part of the negotiation of the artists' contracts or director's contract, or any contract with creative personnel, under certain circumstances it may be possible for the producer to get the creative personnel to accept part of their compensation in the form of a deferment. The obvious advantage of giving a deferment is that it is a fixed sum of money that need not be paid unless there are sufficient gross receipts. In addition, there is no open-end obligation to pay a percentage of net receipts, which could involve substantial sums if the picture is profitable. If the picture is unprofitable, and does not make up the cost of the production with interest, there is never any obligation to pay the deferment. If there is more than one deferment in the picture, either the agreements must provide in which order the deferments are to be paid, or they must provide that the deferments are to be paid pro rata.

In drafting an agreement containing deferment language, the producer will not want to warrant or represent the number of deferments to be given or the total dollar amount of all deferments. On the other hand, the person receiving the deferment will want to know how many other deferments there will be, in what amounts and in what order they are payable.

After all of the discussed deductions, the remaining balance is considered *net receipts*. This sum is sometimes called net profits, and the producer's share of these net profits is the producer's share of gross receipts. In the ordinary production-distribution agreement, usually at least one third of the net receipts (but no more than one half) are payable to the producer, with certain exceptions. Some agreements will provide that if any profit participations are given to members of the cast or creative personnel, these profit participations come out of the producer's share. Other agreements will provide that such participations are taken off the top, so that they are borne by the producer and distributor in proportion to their respective profit participation. For instance, if an artist is entitled to 10% of the profit off the top, that means 90% is left. If the 90% is being split 50-50, then the producer gets

45% and the distributor gets 45%. If the 10% is to come from the producer's share, then the producer would end up with 40% and the distributor with 50%.

When referring to net profit participations, it must be made clear whether a percentage of 100% or some other percentage is meant. If an artist is entitled to 10% of 100% of the net profits, the artist would receive that percentage prior to any other net profit participation deductions. In such case the producer, the distributor, and the other creative personnel would have to divide up the other 90%. If the net profit participation is not phrased as a percentage of 100% of net profits prior to the deduction of any other net profit participations, what the artist may be getting is 10% of what is left after all the other profit participations and other creative personnel are paid. In this way, if all other creative participations were 20% of 100%, then there would be 80% left, and the artist would end up with 10% of 80% or 8%. Usually, artists who are hired to work for a picture get percentages of 100% of the net profits. If, however, the artist or other creative personnel are part of a package, they may be willing to take their percentages on some other basis. This is all a matter of negotiation.

One of the interesting questions that always puzzles outsiders about the motion picture business is why an independent producer should get 33-1/3% to 50% of the net profits. After all, it is argued, an independent producer merely comes with an idea or a literary property, or perhaps a screenplay, and does not bear any of the financial costs of the picture, so he should not be entitled to share in 50% of the profits. Since a finder who puts a deal together may get at most a 4% or 5% finder's fee, it may be hard to understand the rationale of paying an independent producer such a large percentage of the net profits of the picture. A distributor's problem is that no matter how many executives he may hire, they can assess only so many projects, whereas an independent producer can pick and choose until he finds the one project that interests him enough to try and develop it.

In addition, it is an unfortunate fact of the business that very few photoplays ever make net profits. Possibly 10% to 15% of all pictures released ever return enough to pay any net profits. Ordinarily the producer, though hopeful that a profit will be earned, is usually realistic enough to figure that he may very well end up with only his producer's fee.

Sometimes, instead of negotiating for net profits or net receipts, the deal is made on the basis of a multiple of the negative cost of the photoplay; that is, gross receipts are shared after recoupment of a multiple of the negative cost (cost of production). The theory of this is that a picture has to gross a certain multiple of the negative cost before it breaks even. The multiple usually used for pictures costing around $2 million is between 2.5 and 2.8 times the negative cost.

If the negative cost of a picture is $2 million, and the agreed-to multiple is 2.5, when the picture grosses $5 million (which the distributor-financier retains) the distributor will take, with respect to additional gross receipts after $5 million, only a distribution fee, and distribution expenses attributable to the additional gross receipts (usually cooperative advertising costs, taxes, shipping charges, cost of collections, duties, and dubbing costs only)—since the advertising preparation costs and the bulk of the print costs would have been incurred earlier in the ordinary course as part of the multiple computation, and the balance of the gross receipts then becomes net receipts to be shared.

In some cases, the producer, rather than coping with accounting and disputes relating to distribution fees and expenses, will accept a reduced percentage of gross (rather than net) after the multiple. For example, if the producer is to receive 50% of the net after the multiple, and if the distribution fee were on the average 33-1/3%, then if $1.00 of gross were earned after the break-even point, the fee would be 33-1/3 cents. If expenses were 10 cents to 15 cents, then 50% of the balance would be 25 cents. The producer in order to avoid that computation, might accept 25% of the gross after the break-even point. Remember that in figuring net receipts and net profits on the one hand, or a multiple of gross receipts on the other, there is no one fixed break-even point, because each time gross receipts are earned there are distribution expenses attributable to those gross receipts, such as cooperative advertising with respect to theatre exhibitions.

In addition, problems arise regarding the concept of negative cost. In a net receipts deal, the only important difference between

48

a production cost and a distribution expense is that production costs bear interest and overhead and determine the application of a penalty provision. On a multiple deal, each item of negative cost is multiplied. In negotiating a multiple deal, interest should be excluded and any overhead charge (or interest charge, if the distributor will not exclude it) should only be counted one time and not multiplied. The difficulty in a multiple deal is that arguments over allocations remain in computing gross, and arguments over negative cost replace arguments over distribution expenses.

The multiples of the negative cost figures given here as illustrations are not realistic for either very high-budget or very low-budget pictures. This is because the release print expense for a picture costing $10 million and running two hours is the same as it is for picture costing $1 million and running two hours. As a matter of fact, there may not be too much difference in the advertising costs either.

Assuming print and advertising expenditures of $1 million, a picture costing $1 million might break even on a $3 million gross. If the gross receipts are $3 million and the distribution fee is approximately one third, the distribution fee will be $1 million; distribution expenses would be $1 million and the cost of production would be $1 million. In this simplified computation, there is not even an interest charge included. One can readily see that by using a multiple of three—that is, three times the negative cost—the photoplay would almost break even after $3 million of gross receipts.

Again, assuming a picture costs $10 million to produce, and assuming a $21 million gross, the distribution fee of one third would be $7 million, the print and advertising costs might be $4 million and in such event the picture would about break even with a multiple of two. Of course, the bigger the budget for the picture, the more interest runs for each month that goes by before the cost of the production is recouped. Note that the multiple must be based on an evaluation of distribution fees and negative cost. There is no magic formula. Remember also that a multiple for a black-and-white film is only slightly less than that for a color film since, for one reason, print costs may be lower.

from?

In figuring the cost of production of a photoplay, financier-distributors want to include as part of the cost of production all compensation payable to the artist as gross receipts. As far as the the producer is concerned, the distributor will want to treat any sums paid to the artist from gross receipts as additional salary to the artist, and to take the same overhead and interest charge on that salary as on other production costs. If the cost of production (exclusive of the artist's percentage payment) is $1 million and the artist gets 10% of the gross, and the gross is $1 million, then the artist gets $100,000 and the cost of production becomes $1.1 million.

The producer will insist that any gross-receipts deals be paid prior to divisons of net receipts. *(then split distr/prod %)*

In no event should the producer have to pay a percentage of gross receipts to an artist out of the producer's net receipts. This can be totally disastrous. A producer could conceivably be paying money out of his pocket based on gross receipts that he will never receive as net receipts.

(simi see 46- (b)

Chapter Five

OTHER CLAUSES IN THE PRODUCTION-FINANCING AND DISTRIBUTION AGREEMENT

Now that we have examined the concept of gross receipts and how the elusive concept of net receipts is arrived at, it is time to go back to the production-financing-distribution agreement—for convenience called the P-D—and see exactly how various deals are put together and what elements of each deal become important to the producer. The concepts contained in the P-D crop up in many other parts of this book because many other agreements are based on the form of P-D originally entered into.

In this document and associated contracts, a motion picture distributor agrees to finance the production of a motion picture and distribute the completed product. Most of these agreements are many pages long, and most of them contain substantial amounts of *boilerplate* (provisions which through the years have developed to become standard). There are, however, a great number of items in the boilerplate that deserve greater attention than they normally receive, which should be considered from the producer's point of view.

Producer's Compensation

The producer is coming to the distributor with a package. Assuming that the package consists of an option to acquire motion picture rights to a literary property and a screenplay, the first thing that the producer will bargain for and usually receive is repayment for whatever costs the producer has incurred in the project to date. These would include not only the costs for optioning the literary property and having the screenplay written, but other preproduction expenses, including expenses in drafting the option agreement and writer's agreement, location scouting, and other incidental expenses. Sometimes, however, such reimbursement is made only upon the commencement of principal photography.

Although it is unusual, it is possibly worth the effort for the producer to try to obtain some of his compensation in the form of a capital gain. If the motion picture distributor will agree to pay more for the literary property and screenplay than the producer paid, and the producer can convince the Internal Revenue Service that he is not in the business of buying and selling literary property, the difference could be a capital gain and taxable at capital gain rates.

From the distributor's point of view, the distributor wants to keep preproduction costs at a minimum until the distributor is certain the picture is going to be made. In addition, the distributor wants to make sure that the monies being paid to the producer are deemed compensation, so that if there is a breach the distributor has a clear contractual right to damages to recover whatever compensation has been paid. If a large amount of money in excess of actual costs to the producer is attributed to the literary property and screenplay, and the distributor then wants to sue the producer for breach of contract, the distributor may be in the awkward position of claiming that money paid for the literary property was really compensation to the producer. The producer might then be in a position to claim rescission, or a termination of the contract on the theory that if the money for the rights must be repaid, then the rights should be conveyed to the producer, leaving the distributor without any rights in the underlying property.

Because the agreement is ordinarily an agreement to develop a property, most distributors want to make the biggest part of the producer's compensation contingent on the successful development of the picture. In other words, if the film is completed, the producer would then receive the balance of his fee; if the film is not made, the producer receives a limited sum of money for the development. The producer's fee will vary greatly in the amount of cash compensation, profit participation and method of payment. A beginning producer coming to a distributor with a literary property and a screenplay probably can expect between $35,000 and $75,000 as a total fee, but a well-known and experienced producer will receive between $100,000 and $200,000 and up as a fee. Presumably, $10,000 or $15,000 of the fee would be received for development of the property, although sometimes amounts as low as $5,000 are received by the producer. Sometimes the producer must develop the property on speculation. If there is a development fee, no matter what happens to the project, as long as the producer performs, the producer will get at least a minimum fee. An experienced producer may be able to negotiate for a large vested fee or a substantial sum of money to be paid over the preproduction period, whether or not the project goes forward.

Contracting Entity-Artistic Control

Under the format of the P-D, the producer ordinarily provides his own corporation as the contracting entity and engages all of the talent and other personnel. From the distributor's point of view, there are pros and cons to this arrangement.

The distributor may avoid the necessity of entering into union agreements and the problems of doing business in various states, particularly if the picture is going to be produced outside of the major domestic production locales, New York or California. It also becomes easier for the distributor to walk away from the deal if he believes the producer is in breach of the agreement. Since the producer has signed all of the contracts with third parties, he is responsible for all of the contracts, except those that the distributor has been obliged to guarantee. Of course, the distributor may in turn have a responsibility to the producer.

53

If the distributor wants day-to-day control over the course of the production of the photoplay, it makes more sense for it to utilize its own production subsidiary and directly engage the talent. For then, if there are disputes between the producer and the distributor, the rights will be vested in the distributor, and the producer will have a much more difficult time enforcing his rights. If the producer's production company is the contracting entity, all of the distributor's rights are derivative from the rights obtained by the production company and are harder for the distributor to enforce. Cognizant of that fact, distributors take either an assignment of each contract, or a power of attorney from the producer in the P-D to enforce the producer's rights under his contracts.

From the producer's point of view, the producer will wish to use his own company for limiting personal liability and for tax planning. The Internal Revenue Code however subjects one form of personal holding company income—that is, amounts received from contracts for personal services—to a penalty tax. Since the bulk of the corporation receipts in the first year of production may be from personal services of the producer and, therefore, would also be personal holding company income, careful planning in consultation with the producer's accountant and attorney is clearly required.

The producer may have a number of different film projects in development at the same time. When entering into a P-D, one important thing to consider is the setting up of a timetable to insure that at some point the production will proceed past the preproduction stage and into principal photography.

Presumably, the producer will have only one picture in the principal photography stage at a time. Ordinarily, the distributor will insist that the individual producer render exclusive services for six or eight weeks prior to the commencement of principal photography and at least until principal photography is completed. On the other hand, if a producer sets up his timetable and is not successful in completely packaging the project to the distributor's satisfaction within the timetable, insistence upon the producer's adherence to the timetable may force the distributor to abandon the project.

There are various formulas for control of creative elements in the film, ranging from the distributor having the sole and uncontrolled right to approve each element at his sole discretion, to the producer retaining some right of artistic selection and approval that is binding upon the distributor. Ordinarily, however, the distributor, because it is financing the project, will have all artistic approvals.

Another question is which of the parties has the right to select the personnel, whatever the approval rights. Under most P-Ds, the theory is that the producer proposes and the distributor disposes. In other words, the producer makes the selections and the distributor approves or disapproves them.

Sometimes a producer selects a given number of alternative individuals for a function and the distributor must select one. Sometimes a distributor will insist that an actor or director under prior contract to the distributor be used. If the package already includes talent and a director, the removal of one element by the distributor may prejudice the package. Sometimes the distributor will allow the producer to designate minor cast and production personnel, provided salaries are within the budget, the persons are not receiving salaries in excess of their normal rate, no work permits are required, and the personnel are guild members and are experienced in their professions. Generally, if a distributor disapproves a selection of the producer, the producer may make other selections to secure approval, but alternately the P-D must provide that one party or the other has the right to designate.

A sensible way of setting up the P-D is to provide that the producer shall, within a certain number of weeks after delivery of a first draft screenplay, give the distributor a rough budget breakdown. For not more than a few thousand dollars the producer can hire a production man who can assess the first draft of the screenplay and give a rough idea of what it will cost to produce the film, leaving aside, of course, the cost of the principal stars and the director, which are flexible items. The producer must also consider any timetable conflicts inherent in the script.

For instance, if the picture can only be made in the winter time because of the nature of the script, the producer, in planning the project, has to arrange the package with that particular season in mind. If the project requires a particular locale, this can create

55

another problem. No matter what the P-D provides, the more organized the producer is and the more the production is carefully planned, the more likely the distributor will give the producer's effort favorable consideration.

If the distributor approves the producer's budget breakdown, the producer must sign the director and the principal members of the cast. The problem is to coordinate the elements so that they are all ready at the time principal photography is to begin. In addition, while the search for a cast and a director is going on, the producer must have prepared, and the distributor should finance the cost of preparing a detailed budget and a shooting schedule based on the script. Again, there are difficulties. When a director or particular talent is hired, each sometimes wants the privilege of revising the script or at least of polishing it. Changing of scenes will increase script costs, may increase or decrease production costs, and may affect the shooting schedule. Ordinarily the producer comes to the distributor with a proposed film at an estimated price. If the producer has a script, the distributor can make a more sensible evaluation of how much the picture should cost. This evaluation may change because of script revisions and further review of other production details.

At the point at which the distributor approves the major items of the production—the principal cast, the director, budget, script, shooting schedule, locations, and laboratory—the P-D ordinarily provides that the producer's fee becomes vested. In other words, if the distributor decides to cease production of the photoplay after all the approvals have been given (unless due to an Act of God or producer's default), the producer is nonetheless entitled to his fee.

If the producer comes to the distributor with a project and the distributor at any point prior to principal photography disapproves of any of the major elements of the production, the P-D ordinarily provides that the distributor may abandon the project. Some P-Ds afford the distributor the continuing right to abandon the film at any time for any reason. If the distributor notifies the producer under the P-D that it no longer wishes to proceed with the production of the photoplay, the producer has a given period of time—usually from six months to a year—to try to repackage the property and/or obtain other financing. If the producer succeeds, the distributor will return the property to the producer, but the producer must pay the distributor's out-of-pocket costs incurred to that point (usually with interest) and sometimes with the distributor's overhead charge to the film included. As a practical matter, if the producer can make such an outside deal, the distributor may then accept a percentage of its costs expended as a deferment or from profits if the picture is ultimately released.

The P-D will enumerate a number of reasons that the distributor may abandon the project, some of which have nothing to do with the artistic merit of the project. For example, if the distributor has paid for the writing of a number of scripts or extensive revisions, and the production costs have materially escalated, the producer may be directed not to proceed. Some producers feel that if a distributor abandons the film, they have a moral obligation to try to secure the repayment of the distributor's advances. The distributor, in such a case, is grateful if the producer is able to do so, and may be more willing to consider the producer's future projects.

Some distributors provide in their P-Ds that if the distributor abandons production for reasons other than producer's default after principal photography has commenced, the producer does not have the right to buy back the property. In this event, the distributor is liable for contractual costs. The theory behind such a provision is that if the distributor abandons the film after principal photography has commenced, the distributor has invested so much money in the project that no other company would be willing to go forward. From the producer's point of view, he does not want to be in a position where a distributor can declare a project abandoned, eliminate the producer, acquire all rights in the project, and then complete the project without the producer. Agreements generally provide for what is known as a *play or pay* clause, that is, a provision in which the distributor has the option to use or not to use the producer. In any event, he must pay the producer the sums agreed on. Some producers, however, insist that if the picture is made, and the producer or production company is not in breach of the P-D, the producer must have the opportunity to complete the picture. This latter clause in a contract is in all events rare.

57

In assessing his deal, the producer must consider his own overhead. Many producers employ full time a secretary and production staff. While the picture is in the process of being produced, salaries of the secretary and staff, office rental, telephone, and all other overhead items must be paid. The producer will ordinarily ask the distributor to pay or reimburse him for all or a part of that overhead allocable to the picture. If the producer has a number of projects going at one time, there may be an allocation of such expenditures.

Another item considered part of the producer's cost is attorneys' fees. Usually the producer's attorneys will do the work on the production, and the producer negotiates for an item in the budget (usually 1% of the budget, up to a fee of $15,000 or $20,000), which the producer will want paid by the distributor. Sometimes a distributor also adds a charge to the budget for the services of its legal department. Even if the production of a photoplay is abandoned, the distributor usually pays the producer's attorneys a part of the fee, as compensation for the legal work for the literary property, screenplay, and any other agreements entered into before the abandonment. In some cases, the distributor may be reluctant to pay the producer's attorneys for doing the legal work on the assumption that its own legal department can handle the production legal work, and may also be reluctant to pay for the negotiation of the P-D. In this event, the distributor may pay part of the legal fee and the producer would pay part for the work of the producer's attorneys. If the distributor pays no part of the legal fee, the producer must pay it and must take that fact into account in negotiating the deal.

Some of the other basic negotiating points of a P-D relate to matters that also occur in the talent and director's agreements and usually are contained in a separate agreement between the producer and the distributor's production company, including for instance, living expenses paid to the individual producer when rendering services away from his residence, the credit to the individual producer, and other so-called fringes.

Billing Credit to Producer

It is customary that the individual producer of the photoplay

58

receive screen credit (on a separate card from the other credits of the photoplay), and credit in paid advertising. A separate card means that the producer's name is flashed without any other writing on the screen for a period long enough to be read. Various guild requirements maintain that the producer's credit go directly before the credit to the director. This is also true in advertising. The various types of *excluded advertising*, in which the distributor does not have to give the producer credit, will be discussed under talent agreements.

In addition to the credit just mentioned, some producers receive a production credit—*A John Doe Production*—both on the screen and in advertising. Whether or not the producer gets this credit, the size of the credit in relation to other credits and the title of the film, and the position of the credit, are always negotiable points. For tax purposes, and possibly to enhance the corporate image, some producers insist on a credit to the production company on the screen and in advertising. Distributors generally do not object to the screen credit since most producers prefer a production credit with their individual names, and the only purpose of the corporate credit is to give substance to the corporation's activity in producing the photoplay.

A distribution company usually takes a releasing credit (Released by _____), and sometimes a presentation credit is given to an individual executive of the distributor. Occcasionally, one of the chief production executives of the distributor's company will want an executive producer credit. This is all negotiable, and depends on the custom and practice of the distribution company involved. Some distribution companies insist on one thing, others on something else.

Financial Control and Takeover of Production

Most important from the producer's point of view is a contractual commitment by the distributor that the distributor will finance the total cost of the production of the photoplay, will advance all of the monies for distribution of the photoplay, and that the producer will not be required to pay any production or distribution costs, whether or not the picture exceeds the budget. Some distributors do not agree and require the producer to secure

59

completion money (a sum of money that the distributor could call upon if the cost of production exceeds the approved budget).

Ordinarily, the distributor, to insure and supervise financial control, will require a production account to be opened in a bank approved by the distributor, and may insist that all checks from the production account be co-signed by a representative of the producer and a representative of the distributor. A procedure is usually established whereby the producer will advise the distributor how much money is needed for the week's shooting, and the distributor will then deposit that amount of money in the production account. The distributor will ordinarily require a detailed weekly statement of costs and expenses, a schedule of the estimated amount of money needed to complete production of the photoplay, and a daily report indicative of how much of the script and which scenes have been photographed. These breakdowns are prepared on standard production forms by the production manager or the associate producer.

Usually, the individual producer of the photoplay is primarily responsible for packaging the photoplay, making the necessary artistic and budgetary decisions, and keeping everybody happy. The producer will hire an associate producer or a production manager who will do the actual detail work and prepare the financial information and production reports required by the distributor. The production manager will also take care of compliance with the various guild agreements and the other day-to-day matters that affect the production of the photoplay.

If it appears that the cost of production of the photoplay is exceeding the budget, a distributor will ordinarily try to limit exposure. He will retain the right under certain circumstances to take over and assume extensive control of the production of the photoplay. Usually, the P-D will provide that the distributor can take over production of the photoplay if it appears that the cost of production exceeds the budget by a stated amount (such as 10%), or should the production be a certain number of days behind the shooting schedule for any reason other than an Act of God. The number of days will vary from five up.

Usually, days lost as a result of events of an Act of God (or *force majeure*, which concept includes not only Acts of God, but strikes, war, and sometimes any cause outside of the distributor's control) are excluded from the computation. Frequently, the number of days the production is behind in the shooting schedule is directly proportionate to the amount that the production is exceeding the budget. From a distributor's point of view, it should not matter greatly if the production is only a few days behind, if the production winds up on budget. Unfortunately, each day of shooting costs a fixed number of dollars and, if the production is running behind, unless unanticipated savings can be made the cost of production will undoubtedly exceed the final budget.

It is questionable whether or not the right to take over production is meaningful and this may depend on whether the distributor has personnel capable of actually assuming the production of the photoplay. If the distributor does take over production and does complete production, the producer will usually lose the balance of the then unaccrued production fee. In addition, the distributor will generally add a charge to the budget for the production services necessary to complete the film and this charge would also have to be recouped before there would be profits. As a practical matter, if the production did become a runaway production and greatly exceeded the budget, the distributor would in all probability take the position that the producer was in breach of the agreement and would utilize his rights under the default provisions of the contract.

In fact, a distributor's takeover of production of a photoplay is very rare. Ordinarily, the producer will have developed a relationship with the principal members of the cast, the director, and the crew, and will also have the day-to-day knowledge of what is happening which a wise distributor will want to use. There have been some photoplays in which the producer was in fact the only person who knew what was going on and consequently, was virtually indispensible. Most distribution companies do not employ the personnel to take over a production and, therefore, a distributor would be more likely to use the threat of a takeover as a club over the producer's head to effect economies in production or modify the shooting schedule if it appears that the filming is getting out of hand.

A relatively small proportion of all pictures ever make net

profits. When one does, the distributor is usually so happy that he does not want to jeopardize his relationship with the producer by penalizing him because the picture has gone over budget. Because of this, the penalty provisions are not often invoked. On the other hand, if the producer has been wasteful or sloppy, the distributor may feel that even though the picture shows a net profit, the producer should be penalized according to the contract.

To avoid a takeover of the production by the distributor or reduction of producer's profits, most experienced attorneys, in negotiating a P-D, try to exclude certain items in the computation of the cost of production for the purpose of computing whether or not such costs exceeded the budget for the film. Such costs would include those due to *force majeure*, labor or guild increases that take place after the budget has been approved by the distributor, and costs incurred due to the acts of the distributor (e.g., the distributor is late in depositing money in the production account, and for that reason the crew refuses to work, or, if the distributor replaces one of the principals in the cast, and the cost of replacement—plus the costs involved in paying off the original member of the cast—exceeds the allocated costs for that particular role contained in the budget).

— *Completion Bond, Cross-Collateralization, Lien Interest*

With the present-day stress on low-budget productions and on economizing in the making of motion pictures, more and more motion picture companies are insisting on a *completion bond* or completion money being made available. There are certain companies that agree for a fee to provide any costs of producing the photoplay over the approved budget. This subject will be dealt with in a later chapter.

Some distributors may insist that a portion of the producer's fee be withheld until the photoplay is completed. If the photoplay does exceed the budget, the producer's fee is the first money used above the budget. In such event the fee would be recoupable immediately after the distributor has recouped the cost of production of the picture. If a producer has made a prior picture for a distributor and there are net profits due the producer, sometimes a portion of all of the producer's net profits from the first picture are withheld until the completion of the second picture.

In the event that a distributor signs a producer or a production company for a multiple-picture deal, it is quite common for the distributor to insist that all or a substantial part of the net receipts of each picture be cross-collateralized. This means that if there are net receipts payable to the producer on the first picture, those net receipts would be withheld, and the distributor would utilize the net receipts to recoup the cost of production of the second picture, the third from the profits of the first and second, etc. From the point of view of the producer, this procedure is almost certain to insure that the producer will never receive any net profits, since it is most unlikely that a producer can make two or three pictures consecutively that will cumulatively show enough net profits under this formula. On the other hand, the fact that a producer has two or three pictures with one distributor would enhance the producer's reputation in the business and also insure the producer of guaranteed sums in producer's fees. If net receipts of a prior picture are used to recoup production costs, the interest charge on the unrecouped production costs will be less. In addition, while the films are in production, the distributor for that period of time would possibly be covering all or part of the producer's overhead and be giving the producer enough capital to commence other projects. One trouble with multi-picture deals, of course, is that if the first picture is financially successful, the producer wants to renegotiate the contract terms, while if the first picture is not successful, the distributor may not want to have anything further to do with the producer. In any event the producer whose net receipts are cross-collateralized should provide for the periodic release of some net receipts or he may never receive money as long as one of the pictures is potentially un-recouped.

A brief review of the important financial bargaining points the producer has to be concerned about follows:

1. His percentage of net receipts and the computation thereof;
2. His producer's fee and manner of payment;
3. His living expenses;
4. His production overhead;

5. Some guarantees as to adjustment of profit and takeover rights by the distributor;

6. The proportion of the producer's fee that in any event is vested, whether or not the project is completed;

7. A schedule of the course of events from preproduction through delivery.

The attorney negotiating for the producer in a P-D must carefully consider certain additional clauses in the usual production-distribution agreement. One such clause consists of certain artificial charges such as a distributor's general overhead charge, which a distributor may wish to include in the cost of production of the photoplay. Some of these charges have been considered in the chapter dealing with the computation of net receipts. Other charges may be partially artificial, such as the studio facilities, which is a percentage of the budget overhead charge. It may be difficult to determine how much of the charge represents costs that would have to be paid in any event, depending on the studio facilities available and the price of the facilities. As was previously mentioned, some distribution companies will insist on a distributor's representative who will countersign checks, be present throughout shooting, and generally keep the distributor informed as to whether the production is exceeding the budget or running behind schedule. If there is a representative, he usually starts work a few weeks prior to principal photography, and continues until one or two weeks after completion of principal photography. This is not considered an artificial charge, in that the distributor normally pays the representative the sum set forth in the budget. It is, nevertheless, a charge that the producer may feel is unnecessary because it is his responsibility to bring the picture in on time and on budget.

Another item of concern to the producer and his attorney are the provisions relating to the consequences in the event of a default or a termination of the P-D for reasons other than producer's breach. Before discussing the relative positions of the parties in the event of the default of the other, some time should be spent in considering the structure and format of the P-D from the producer's point of view.

Some distribution companies provide in their contracts that ownership of all rights and the copyright in the photoplay are held by the distributor, and that the producer has an interest only in sums equal to net profits derived from the photoplay. The distributor's position is that the ownership of the copyright and all rights would place the distributor in a better negotiating position in the event of a dispute between it and the producer. In addition, the investment tax credit is payable to the holder of legal title to the film, although there is some belief that the credit will be paid to the investor, whether or not the investor has legal title.

Some distributors permit the copyright in the photoplay to be in the sole name of the producer, subject to the distributor's rights under the P-D. From the producer's point of view, such procedure would give the production company more substance, and anything that gives the production company more substance benefits the producer.

In order to secure the monies advanced to the production company, the distributor, in lieu of copyright ownership, may take a security interest in the picture, including the copyright and the literary property as well as the preprint film material. The distributor may then consider the monies advanced to the producer as production loans and receive interest on those loans. Each time a sum of money is advanced to the producer under this arrangement, the distributor receives a promissory note for that loan from the producer. Usually such an arrangement would provide that in the event the distributor has not recouped the cost of production by a specified date, the distributor could foreclose the producer's interest in the photoplay. Under such a foreclosure proceeding, the distributor would bid for the picture at the amount of the unrecouped negative cost, which is generally so large there would be little likelihood that the distributor would be outbid for the picture. This is known as a *dry mortgage*, since the producer is not liable for repayment of the loan and the promissory notes are repayable solely from film receipts.

This kind of arrangement would make the P-D a loan transaction and would have certain inherent dangers for both the producer and the distributor. The producer naturally would want to be protected against a foreclosure that might eliminate his interest in net profits, particularly if a new form of distribution later comes along that might generate large sums of money for the picture. In addition, the producer certainly does not want to sign or have his company sign promissory notes which may be negotiated to third parties or on which payment may be demanded if there is an alleged breach of the contract.

On the other hand, the difficulty from the distributor's point of view is that if the producer owns the picture and copyright interest in the picture, and there is a dispute between the producer and the distributor, the distributor may find it difficult to foreclose its lien in order to enforce its rights under the security documentation.

Another possibility is for the copyright to be held by the producer and distributor as tenants in common. The distributor would still have a security interest with respect to the producer's right, title, and interest in the film, but the distributor, as a tenant in common of the copyright and thus the underlying rights, would have more protection in the event of a dispute with the producer.

Before discussing what may happen in the event that there is a default by the production company, the contractual responsibilities of the production company should be considered. Bear in mind that in most cases the distributor will have final say with respect to all artistic controls, but it is still the production company's responsibility to select the principal members of the cast and production elements. As previously noted, it is also the producer's responsibility to prepare the budget and to see to it that the screenplay is written. However, the fact that persons not the producer or an employee of the production company may not perform under their contracts with the production company should not be considered a breach by the production company. In other words, if a screenwriter agrees to deliver a script by July 1, and does not deliver until August 1, the screenwriter may be in breach, but the production company would not be in breach of its P-D with the distributor.

Insurance

During principal photography of the photoplay, the producer has various other responsibilities, all of which are spelled out in the P-D. One such responsibility is to obtain necessary insurance. Initially, the producer obtains a form of insurance known as an *errors and omissions* policy, which protects the distributor (and usually the producer) against claims by third parties for copyright infringement, libel and slander, unfair competition, and other similar causes of action. Such claims might arise because of defamatory or infringing material contained in the underlying literary property or the screenplay (such as someone's being photographed without his consent, or a location release [permission from places depicted in the film or places in which filming is taking place] not being obtained; or something of similar nature). A production manager will generally know when and from whom releases are required.

The issuance of such insurance is usually conditioned on counsel for the production company or the distributor, as the case may be (depending on who takes out the insurance) being reasonably experienced in film matters and taking reasonable care in clearing rights. Most distributors will carry errors and omissions insurance under "blanket" policies (including coverage for a number of its pictures), and the distributor would get a lower premium rate than the producer could if the producer tried to get insurance on only one picture. Generally, the distributor will pay a fixed premium for each picture endorsed under the policy. If a lump sum of money is paid, no matter how many pictures are endorsed under the policy, an allocation of this cost would have to be made for each particular production. Some distributors take advantage of the blanket rate but charge the company with the higher per picture premium.

A producer will want to be included as a named insured under the errors and omissions policy. If the producer is a named insured, then the insurance company waives any rights of subrogation it may have against the production company for any claim covered by insurance which might be deemed a breach of the P-D by the producer. Some distributors agree to this inclusion, and ordinarily there is no extra charge from the insurance company if the producer is endorsed on the policy as one of the insured. Even if there is an extra charge the distributor may assume it, or if the distributor will not, then the producer may want to pay for the protection. The insurance company will cover loss to the insured arising from any claim up to the stated policy limits, which are usually at least $250,000 for one claim and $500,000 for all claims. Of course, higher limits can be obtained.

The insurance company will not cover losses incurred as a result of an injunction against the distribution of the film, but will reimburse the distributor for the cost of prints and advertising. There remains a considerable gap in the coverage because if there is an injunction, the distributor may end up with a picture that cannot be distributed at all. By the same token, an insurance company does not want to assume the open-ended risk. The insurance company will ordinarily require a copy of the title report with respect to the literary property.

The producer's responsibility under the insurance policy includes checking fictional names and locations to make sure there are no real-life similarities, getting permission to photograph people and locations appearing in the script, and permission to use real names of people, and places or products mentioned in the script. These are generally handled by the production manager.

Another important form of insurance is *cast insurance*. Again, many of the distributors have their own blanket cast insurance policy whereby each picture is endorsed on the policy. The cost of this insurance is generally based on a percentage of the cost of production of the photoplay, and will also depend upon the number of weeks of principal photography. Cast insurance ordinarily begins four weeks prior to commencement of principal photography and continues to the end of principal photography. Under the cast insurance policy, the basic premium will cover a minimum of six persons, usually the director and five of the principal members of the cast. If more people must be insured, the cost of the premium increases. If any member of the cast covered by cast insurance should die, or become disabled or disfigured, the insurance company will pay the amount of the loss above a stated deductible amount. A condition of cast insurance is that each member of the cast covered by the policy receive a medical examination conducted by a doctor selected by the insurance company. If a member of the cast does not pass the insurance examination, he may be excluded from the policy; a higher deductible amount may be fixed, an increased premium may be charged, or a particular ailment excluded.

Cast insurance policies raise some very complicated questions. For instance, for a person with a recurring injury, was there, in fact, one injury, with one deductible amount taken into consideration, or two separate injuries with two deductibles? This question could also apply in the case of an illness. Another difficulty involves actually proving the amount of the loss, and the success in maintaining a claim will depend upon the ability of the production supervisor and the production accountants to itemize elements of loss flowing from the inability to perform. For example, if the shooting of the photoplay must be rescheduled or shot in a different sequence because one of the members of the cast is ill, a determination must be made as to how much time has actually been lost, how much additional cost has been incurred, whether payments to other cast members who are on standby because of the illness should be included, and whether a scene must be reshot or a double be used.

The insurance policies will contain a clause which provides that the losses must be due "directly" to the injury, and if there is some intervening factor which also contributes to the loss, the insurance company need not pay. Theoretically, if, on the day that a member of the cast became ill, there was a fire and all of the sets were destroyed, there would be no coverage and no payment under the cast insurance policy. The fire would be the intervening factor which contributed to the loss, and there presumably would be no claim.

On the other hand, a member of the cast may become disabled for 20 days, during which period snow is in fact on the ground and snow sequences are to be photographed. If at the end of the 20 day period, there is no more snow and the sequences have to be shot elsewhere at substantially greater costs, it must be determined whether the insurance company is liable for the greater cost of shooting the snow sequences in another location, or is only liable for the losses that would have occurred had it been possible to shoot the snow sequences in the original location. The insurance company takes the latter view. Disputes arise because a single form of insurance policy cannot cover many of the potential situations.

It is possible to obtain cast insurance covering a period longer than the time of principal photography, plus a stated number of weeks prior to principal photography on payment of an additional premium. Under certain circumstances the cost is worthwhile, particularly if expenses are being incurred well in advance of principal photography and the film is a showcase for an actor or director. In lieu of cast insurance, life insurance (which is much cheaper) is sometimes obtained for the period to cover part of the risk.

If an actor who has completed half of his role suddenly dies, the cost of reshooting the entire film with another actor might well exceed the cost of terminating the production in the middle. The insurance company would, in this case, prefer to terminate, but the producer and the distributor might want to proceed with a new actor. In the latter case, the insurance company would take the position that it was liable only for the costs incurred had the production in fact been terminated. This is not an unreasonable position, and characterizes the uncertainty of protection afforded. Of course, no one will insure a producer against an actor quitting before completion of the film.

A third type of insurance usually obtained is *negative insurance*. This insurance protects the negative of the photoplay against damage or destruction. All laboratories limit their liability for any damage to a negative to the replacement cost of the raw stock of the negative; they are not liable for the production cost of the film itself. Usually there is an amount deductible from the coverage with negative insurance. If the negative is damaged, the production staff and the laboratory usually end up arguing as to who was responsible for the defective negative footage. Negative insurance coverage usually is effected at the commencement of principal photography, and is maintained until a duplicated negative is manufactured. After that, coverage is discontinued because it is very expensive. Ordinarily, the original picture negative and the duplicate negative are kept in separate places, so if one is damaged by fire or other accident, the other probably would not be harmed. The producer and distributor take the chance that there will not be a simultaneous disaster at both places of storage.

Other insurance purchased for a motion picture will usually include: workmen's compensation; aviation insurance, if applicable; fire, theft, and property insurance; third party liability; and insurance that may be required for any special risks involved in the production. There are a number of insurance brokers who specialize in entertainment insurance, and they furnish information concerning the types of insurance that should be obtained for a particular production.

Union Contracts

Most P-Ds provide that the independent production company will be responsible for entering into any collective bargaining agreements required to produce the picture. Most unions require a bond from the production company or a lien on the picture as security to insure payment of salaries and residuals, but in some cases the union will accept the distribution company's guarantee of payment. In this case, the distributor agrees to make residual payments directly to the guild and a bond or lien may not be required.

Because of the relatively few motion pictures presently being produced in the U.S., there is some question about the bargaining strength of the various guilds. It is sometimes possible to get some form of concession from the various guilds involved in production of the photoplay, either because of published concessions for low-budget films, or through separate negotiation. The concessions are generally verbal and usually the subject of agreement between the production manager and the union officials, and they vary from film to film. Ordinarily, the various union agreements are signed "as is" by the production company. Which concessions to bargain for depends upon the special problems involved in a film. For instance, if there is a lot of night shooting, one might negotiate a later starting time to reduce the overtime rates. The question of which guild agreements, if any, to sign depends upon which guilds have jurisdiction, and that depends upon the place in which the film is being produced. If a film is being produced at more than one location, there may be a problem, if more than one guild claims jurisdiction. In this era of low-budget films, some producers wish to avoid paying union scale wages altogether.

The most powerful union in the U.S. film industry is generally considered to be the International Association of Theatre and Stage Employees (IATSE). This guild permits (and obligates) a

71

production company using IATSE personnel to use a production seal of approval on the main title of the film. Traditionally, when a union discovers that a motion picture company is producing a film with non-union help, the union will either picket the production or, through the Projectionists' Union, refuse to exhibit the film at theatres when it is released. It is true that many photoplays have recently been produced and exhibited in the U.S. which have not had the IATSE seal. Whether or not IATSE will permit this situation to continue is questionable.

A smaller union, but competitive to IATSE, is NABET (National Association of Broadcast Engineers and Technicians). This union is more flexible in altering working hours and making similar concessions. It has been said, however, that IATSE would react more strongly against a film showing a NABET bug (union seal) than against one showing no bug at all.

The safest course for a producer is to sign any union agreements necessary to insure that the production of the photoplay will be uninterrupted. If there is going to be any budgetary short-cut taken to avoid union requirements, it should have the distributor's prior approval. If the distributor is a major distributor, it will have its own collective agreements with the various unions. The distributor will be reluctant to do anything that might interfere with its relationship with the unions, for it would affect its other films. However, such a distributor might not hesitate to distribute a completed film made with no union help and not financed by the distributor.

Productions Outside U.S.

Sometimes substantial savings in the cost of producing a film may result if it is produced outside of the U.S. Labor costs are usually lower although the differential has been shrinking in recent years. For instance, it has been said that recording the musical portion of films in England costs approximately half as much as the U.S. If recording were to take place in Yugoslavia or Italy, the costs would be even lower.

If the story of the photoplay will allow the film to be produced at any one of a number of locations, the producer's bargaining position with the unions will be much stronger than if the film

72

must be shot at a particular location, as the producer can shoot the film elsewhere if he does not get the local concessions he wants. In considering the location of the production of the film, it should be remembered that some countries have various forms of financial aid to encourage local film productions.

In England, this form of film aid is called the EADY plan. Under the EADY plan, theatres pay a certain percentage of box office receipts to a central agency. At the end of the year, the percentage is divided and distributed in proportion to the box office receipts of each film qualifying for the EADY plan. Depending on the cost of production of the photoplay, the EADY plan aid can amount to as much as 40% of the cost of production.

There are only a few principal requirements for qualifying under the EADY plan. A least 80% of the salary costs of the film must be paid to British nationals. In computing the 80%, two exceptions can be taken into consideration. For example, two American stars (or a star and the director) can be hired whose salaries are not counted in computing the 80%.

Another requirement is that the film be photographed in a British studio or in Great Britain. If filming will be done outside of Great Britain, it is permissible for a British crew to work at the location. The producer must determine whether or not the benefits of the EADY money outweigh the costs of flying a British crew to a particular location and housing them there.

Similar plans exist in Italy and in France with generally similar requirements. These countries also require that the photoplay be photographed in the original language of the aid countries, but there are exceptions to this rule.

One practice is to set up a co-production between companies of two nationalities. This is allowed under various conventions between two countries which provide for co-productions such as British-Italian or French-Italian. Ordinarily, the production company of one country will put up the bulk of the money and provide most of the personnel, and the other country will put up the balance of the money and personnel. Each production company reserves its territory to itself, and net receipts are shared in proportion to the amount of capital advanced or credit loaned. By arranging this sort of a co-production, it is sometimes possible to take advantage of and have the film qualify for film aid in both countries.

In Italy, there is not only an equivalent of the EADY plan but also an additional payment called the *quality premium*, which is paid to films that the Italian government deems of unique artistic quality. The payments received by a producer in Italy and in France are generally substantially less than the payments that can be obtained in England. In addition, the French payments must be used for future productions in France. Therefore, from the production company's point of view, trying to secure French aid is difficult unless either the production company or the distribution company plans to do additional filming in France or can discount the aid to another production company.

All forms of film aid become gross receipts of the film, and generally the distribution company does not take a distribution fee on such gross receipts. If the distribution company wants a particular film to qualify for aid, the producer must be careful to see that all the technical requirements of securing the aid are met.

Cutting, Editing, and Delivery of Completed Film

Most P-Ds require that the photoplay shall not contain salacious, obscene, controversial, or political matter, and that the completed photoplay will be able to obtain a rating other than an X (persons under age 17 not admitted) or an R (parent or guardian must accompany anyone under 17) rating from the Motion Picture Association. If the producer expects that the photoplay will be of a political or controversial nature, or will contain scenes that will result in an X or an R rating, this provision of the P-D must be modified. Some agreements provide that the producer must film cover shots of any scenes that might cause the film to be given an X or R rating. The cover scenes would be filmed without the objectionable material. In this event, the budget would have to provide for the extra cost of the cover shots. On the other hand, sometimes the "questionable" scenes are added later to help the marketability of the film.

Most P-Ds usually give the distributor the right to cut and edit the photoplay. However, under the Director's Guild of America Minimum Basic Agreement, the director has the right to at least one cut of the photoplay, and the producer, depending on his bargaining position, may want additional cutting rights after the director has edited the film. The producer may request a public preview after the first cut and the right to further edit the film based on the audience reaction at the preview. Sometimes there are two previews, with cuts after each one. In the discussion of the director's agreement, some of the specific provisions relating to cutting rights are set forth.

Some producers obtain the right of *final cut*. In other words, the distributor must release the photoplay as delivered to the distributor by the producer. Even in situations in which the producer has the right of final cut, the distributor will ordinarily have the right to cut the photoplay for censorship and the requirements of television exhibition. The distributor will also have the right to insert or authorize the insertion of commercials (for instance, for television and even theatrical release in some foreign countries).

Another responsibility of the producer is to make sure that the billing credits, both on the main title and on paid advertising, conform to the contractual and guild requirements with talent and production personnel. Usually, the producer prepares a summary of the screen and advertising credit obligations that is reviewed by both the producer and the distributor.

The P-D requires the producer to deliver to the distributor the negative of the completed film together with certain preprint materials such as the independent music and effects track, one dialogue track, additional footage not used, and a textless background of the main and end titles. Delivery of all of these items are conditions that must be met before a distributor will accept delivery of a film. From the producer's point of view, the extent of the list is relatively unimportant since, although the cost of the materials increase the cost of production, the distributor bears the cost of the materials; more important, the budget must make provision for the cost of all of the required materials.

Ordinarily, the distributor will also want to designate the laboratory that does the processing of the negative materials, and also the laboratory that manufactures the positive (release) prints of

75

the film. Most distributors have blanket agreements with a particular laboratory and will ordinarily get lower prices than a particular producer may obtain for processing one photoplay. However, a producer may have a strong opinion about the quality of the work of a particular laboratory, and most blanket agreements between a distributor and a laboratory will give the distributor the right to have the printing done at another laboratory if the producer insists upon it. Whether or not the producer can insist upon selecting the laboratory depends upon his bargaining position and the reputation of the particular laboratory that the distributor wishes to use.

The more elements of production over which the distributor grants the producer sole discretion, the more likely it is that the distributor can claim that the producer is in default under the terms of the P-D. One question is whether a producer should insist upon having the contract recite specific rights, which the distributor would ordinarily give the producer as a matter of business procedure anyway. If the producer succeeds in obtaining an enumeration of specific rights in the agreement and does not exercise those rights properly, it is easy for the distributor to claim a breach. If, however, the producer does not insist on an enumeration of rights and mistakenly relies on the usual business practices of the distributor, the producer may lose all artistic controls in the production. If the distributor, contrary to usual practice, decides to take an active part in production, it would be hard for the distribution company to claim successfully that the producer breached the contract if the distributor has all approvals, certain rights of designations and has in essence approved everything as the film has progressed.

It is always prudent for the producer initially to clear in writing all important decisions with the distribution company. Once the distributor approves something, it is virtually impossible for it later to claim a breach based on what it has approved.

Termination Rights

Leaving aside the question of security documentation (documents securing the distributor's interest in the film), and its

76

enforceability, all P-Ds will provide for rights of termination and rights in the event of default. Most P-Ds provide that the distributor can terminate the production of a film at any time and for any reason. The producer may insist that there may be a termination only in the event of an Act of God, the death or disability of the director or principal member of the cast, or a run-away production (to be discussed further), indefinitely prolonging production for which insurance is not available, or some contractual provisions giving the distributor the right to terminate upon the occurrence of specific events. The distributor, however, ordinarily fights for the right to terminate for any reason whatsoever and at its own discretion.

Most distribution agreements will provide that if there is a termination, the distributor will own the photoplay (unless there are abandonment or turn-around rights for the producer to buy back the picture), but the distributor agrees to pay when due any costs expended or incurred by the producer prior to the date of termination. If there is a termination, the P-D must provide answers to the following questions: Is the producer entitled to the full producer's fee even if the film is terminated in mid-production, or only that portion of the producer's fee which has accrued prior to the date of termination? (Note that much of the producer's fee may become payable only upon the delivery of the film to the distributor.) Is the producer entitled to net profits if the distribution company later makes the film? If the distribution company is going to remake the film, does the producer have the option to be the producer of the film? If so, on what terms?

There is no easy solution to these questions and all of them are the subject of serious prolonged bargaining. Ordinarily, if there is a termination, the distributor will have incurred so much cost that it is most unlikely that the production would ever commence again. In the event of a termination, the distributor would argue that it had suffered a great financial loss and that the producer should share part of that loss by receiving only that portion of the production fee accrued.

In the event of a default by the producer, there are other factors to consider. Most P-Ds provide that in the event of a default, the distributor in addition to remedies at law or equity, has any or all of the following rights: to terminate production and terminate the agreement; to take over production of the film from the producer; to offset any damages against any sums otherwise due the producer under the agreement or any other agreements between the parties; not to pay the balance of the producer's fee; and not to pay any costs of producing the film after the breach. Note that if the distributor does not have to finance the balance of the cost of production of the photoplay, the production company is still responsible for payment of all obligations under all of its agreements with artistic and technical personnel, as well as studio facilities, etc. In addition, if the producer's production company has an ownership interest in the film and the distributor has taken a lien on the producer's interest in the film, has filed appropriate security documentation, and has received promissory notes in connection with the financing of the cost of production of the film, then the distributor may exercise its contractual right to foreclose the lien on the photoplay and declare the notes payable.

To what extent may a producer whittle away at these rights of the distributor? Many distribution companies will agree that their rights in the event of a default will not be exercised unless the breach or default is material. Producers request a grace period to cure a breach or default. From the point of view of the distributor, it is senseless to permit a grace period with respect to certain defaults. For instance, if a producer becomes disorderly on the set every day, what point is there in giving him a five-day period to cure each separate default? On the other hand, there are certain breaches of warranty or breaches of agreement which could conceivably be corrected within a grace period without prejudicing the distributor.

If the production company has substantial assets, the producer must not allow the production company to be potentially responsible, even if there is a default, for all or a portion of the cost of producing the photoplay, for this is the very thing for which the distributor was supposed to assume responsibility. Similarly, no individual producer should sign a personal guarantee of the obligations of the production company.

On the other hand, the distributor can argue that because of the producer's breach, it has incurred production costs which other-

78

wise would not have been incurred. These costs, at least, should be paid by the producer. For this reason, many production companies are really no-asset corporations, and, presumably, if the distributor, exercised its rights under the default provision of the contract, or attempted to enforce repayment of the production costs by calling due its promissory notes, the production company would be totally unable to pay. In that event, like it or not, the distributor would probably have to pay the production costs itself, even if it could claim the obligation was the producer's; the distributor could not afford to jeopardize its continuing relationship with the various talent agencies that provide talent, and the various unions involved.

Using a no-asset corporation may limit the possibilities for the producer to effect tax planning, but unless the production company has enough bargaining position to change the P-D so as to eliminate liability for production costs in the event of breach, a no-asset company should be used. Many P-Ds are initially drafted in such a way that the producer, if he did not request substantial changes, would technically be in breach of the agreement as he finished affixing his signature to it. Sometimes these agreements cannot be negotiated, or negotiated only with great difficulty, if the producer has a weak bargaining position.

Most P-Ds provide that if the individual producer is an officer, director, or stockholder of the production company, then a breach by the production company is a breach by the individual producer. In some P-Ds, the obligations of the individual producer are spelled out in the agreement, and the individual producer individually signs, in effect, a ratification of the agreement. In other agreements, the individual producer will enter into a formal producer's agreement (the form of which is discussed in Chapter 9) with his own production company. In those instances, the distributor will usually try to provide that a breach of one agreement is, at the distributor's election, a breach of both. This will also make the producer individually liable, although the concept of damages under an individual producer's agreement differs from a P-D. Ordinarily the extent of the damages is not spelled out in the agreement, but must be proved in a lawsuit, whereas in the P-D, liability is fixed in terms of repayment of production costs.

79

Although the producer will try to shirk individual responsibility, the distributor will argue that the production company is but a tool for the producer's benefit, and anything that the production company does must be the producer's responsibility.

Note that there may be certain breaches by third parties involved in the production which occur during production but which are not the responsibility of a production company. For instance, if an actor defaults under the terms of his contract with a production company, that certainly is not the production company's responsibility. Similarly, if there is an event of *force majeure*, that is not the production company's responsibility. Ordinarily, there is so much at stake for the distributor, and the consequences of a dispute between the producer and distributor are so potentially disruptive of the shooting of a film, that, if at all possible—even if the producer is in breach—the distributor will either rely on some other production personnel to complete the production of the film, or will wait until the production of the photoplay is completed before exercising its rights or making a claim against the producer.

Producers Warranties and Remedies of Parties for Breach

The usual P-D calls for the producer to make numerous warranties. Under ordinary circumstances, the distribution company will acquire the producer's rights in the literary property from the producer. In the course of that acquisition, as part of the P-D, the distribution company will want the producer to make the same warranties that the author gave to the producer when the producer acquired rights in the literary property and the script. The producer will argue that he cannot make such a warranty except to the best of his knowledge, information, and belief, or that only the author should make the warranty. The distributor will argue that the producer must warrant that which he is conveying.

A producer must make other warranties that he will acquire the usual rights from the cast, crew and other personnel, not create liens, obtain proper releases, etc. If the producer has followed the customary clearance techniques during filming, and if the agreements with cast—and, where necessary, crew—have all been approved by the distributor, and the distributor's attorneys have

80

approved all the contractual forms to be used in connection with the production of the photoplay, the producer does not have to worry too much about his warranties.

If there is a breach of warranty, the distributor will want the producer to indemnify the distributor against any claims and the right to settle or dispose of the claims. The same principles with respect to indemnification, rights to settle and defend, etc., that were applicable in the discussion of the acquisition of rights in a literary property from an author apply here. However, the distributor will have obtained insurance covering the claim, and if the producer is a named insured on the policy, the insurance company will not have any right to recover its loss from the producer in the event of a claim for infringement, libel, or slander which would be covered by insurance.

The producer's remedies against the distributor, if the distributor breaches, are severely limited in the P-D. Almost all P-Ds provide that in the event the distributor breaches or is in default, the producer can only sue for money damages, and the producer does not have the right to rescind the agreement or the rights granted the distributor in the P-D to enjoin or restrain the distribution of the photoplay or the advertising of the photoplay. To the distributor, this clause is an absolute necessity because of its risk involved—namely that if the producer claims a breach, and if the distributor disputes the claim and loses in court, the producer can prevent the film from being completed or distributed. If the distributor has invested substantial sums of money in financing the production of the film, the distributor will want to protect that investment. In addition, the distributor may have had to mortgage all or part of its interest in the film in order to obtain financing, and if this is the case, the financier will insist that the distributor have the unrestricted right to distribute the film, free from any threat of termination or injunction. Obviously, the financier is prejudiced if the distributor's rights in a film, and hence, the financier's collateral can be terminated.

Actually, the basic defaults a distributor can commit, prior to the distribution of the film, are the failure to furnish money, or the failure to accord proper billing credits. If the distributor fails to furnish money, either in financing the film or in paying pro-

81

ducer's fees, there is nothing to prevent the producer from ceasing to render services. As stated, it is very difficult for the distributor not to continue to finance the production of the film. Once photography of the photoplay has started, so much money has been committed by it that, unless there is some rare catastrophe which is covered by insurance, it is almost inconceivable that a distributor would walk away from a film in the middle unless it runs out of money. However, if a producer is relegated to a suit for the money damages, the producer must, at the very least, be certain that the distributor could pay a judgment. Even then, if the producer has spent time in developing a project and is relying mainly on net receipts from distribution of the film for compensation and is accepting a small fixed fee, the potential net receipts may be too speculative for a court to award damages based on net receipts not received. To the extent that an award in money damages cannot compensate a producer fully, should not the producer have some rights of termination if a distributor stops financing or becomes bankrupt? The producer's argument is well taken, but most producers do not have the bargaining power to impose this view on distributors.

Most disagreements about billing credit are due to inadvertent mistakes of the distributor. But what if the producer's credit is omitted or not given proper size or prominence on the screen or in advertising? The distributor argues that it should not be in a position in which the advertising can be enjoined if it is incorrect. The logic of this is that if a distributor is in the process of commencing distribution of the photoplay, and the advertising is enjoined, it would be impossible to prepare new ads in time for the advertising to be useful to promote specific engagements of the film. In the meantime advertising space already committed would have to be paid for.

There may be an even bigger problem in connection with the main title. Once the negative has been prepared, and the other preprint materials have been manufactured from the negative and the picture has been cut, edited, and scored, and release prints have been manufactured, if there is a mistake in the credit on the release prints, it would be necessary to have new negative material prepared correcting the credit, to manufacture new print material from the new negative materials, ship each release print to the

82

laboratory, and have the new material spliced onto the existing print. This is a fantastically costly process, and an expense that a distributor would not wish to incur. In addition, if a new credit had to be added, it might disrupt the continuity of the action under the titles or the scoring geared to the existing credits.

From the producer's point of view, it is very difficult, if not impossible, to prove money damages resulting from a failure to accord proper credits in advertising. Fortunately, for all concerned, unless the relationship between two parties is so bad that the distributor becomes completely vindictive, it is most unusual that a distributor would fail to accord any billing credit contractually called for to the producer. Most usually, billing credits are or should be spelled out with such exactitude that no argument can arise. For this reason, subjective words such as "prominence" are conducive to dispute. The problem of billing credits may be compounded by the fact that although the distributor may put in the press book (furnished to exhibitors from which ads for newspapers can be made) suggested advertising showing official billing as contracted, theatrical exhibitors may and do ignore the billing obligations and prepare their own advertising omitting certain credits. Even though the distributor has a contractual right to tell the exhibitor to honor the credits appearing in the ads and use the form of ad requested by the distributors, the distributor may be unwilling to enforce those provisions. After all, it is to the distributor's interest to have the exhibitor exhibit the photoplay, and the distributor does not wish to alienate its customers. In addition, the engagement may be near its end. As a practical matter, a distributor might believe a suit against an exhibitor would accomplish nothing.

Most distributors insert provisions in the P-D stating that a breach by an exhibitor or licensee of the billing is not a breach by them. Again, producers' efforts to obtain monetary damages may be difficult to accomplish. Even so, the producer may not be able to bargain for greater remedies, including various forms of injunctive relief.

If the distributor fails to account or pay after commencing distribution, the same principles and arguments apply. If the producer can terminate a P-D or restrain distribution, the distributor may, besides jeopardizing its investment in the film, breach its own agreements with licensees and subdistributors. One resolution is to make a termination subject to the assumption of existing agreements. Can the producer fulfill the obligations under such agreements? Most distributors (especially those who finance production) will strenuously resist any provision that might terminate distribution rights.

Security Documents and Consequences of Exceeding Budget

Let us now consider the various security documents that form part of a typical P-D. Security documents are those documents pursuant to which a lien on the film, the literary, dramatic and musical material, and the preprint and print material may be acquired by a distributor to secure the distributor's investment in a film. The purpose of the lien is to give the distributor a right to foreclose on any ownership interest of the producer in the film if the producer breaches the P-D, or becomes insolvent or bankrupt. The right of foreclosure protects the distributor's distribution rights.

Of course, if the distributor is the sole copyright proprietor, and owns all rights in the film, the producer is only entitled to a sum of money measured by his net receipt percentage participation, as well as, of course, his producer's fee. In this format, the producer would have no ownership interest in the photoplay, and the distributor would not need any security documentation, since all rights in the film, and all literary, musical and physical film materials would be in the distributor and owned by the distributor, and the producer would own nothing. Otherwise, the distributor will want a lien on the producer's ownership interest in the photoplay. The lien is usually created by a security agreement in which the producer grants the distributor a lien on all of the producer's right, title, and interest in the film as security for the distributor's financing the film. The distributor would thus acquire the producer's interest in the film if the producer defaults under the P-D, breaches any warranty or representation in the security agreement, or the photoplay does not recoup its negative cost within a given period of time. In most other respects, a secutity agreement for a film would follow the form of security agreement used for other purposes.

84

A financing statement under the Uniform Commercial Code (UCC) (a requirement for making the security interest valid against persons who would otherwise not have notice) is ordinarily filed where the producer is incorporated, is principally doing business, and where principal photography of the photoplay will occur. The financing statement filing under the UCC gives third parties notice of the existence of a security interest in the film and gives notice that the secured party has acquired a lien. Usually, the UCC financing statement refers to the agreement which must be consulted for specifics. Ordinarily, the two jurisdictions involved will be New York and California. Since the copyright act provides for the recording of mortgages, there is a question as to whether or not the federal law preempts the field so as to make the whole process of filing UCC financing statements for copyrighted materials meaningless, even though the copyright act does not provide for foreclosure of mortgages.

Since state law may provide for the foreclosing of mortgages and since no attorney wants to set new milestones in litigation, the practical answer to the problem is to record the required documents in both places. Therefore, in addition to the security agreement and the UCC financing statement, a short-form mortgage of chattels and copyright is generally prepared and filed in the U.S. copyright office. The typical chain of title, therefore, which a copyright search might reveal, would show a literary property short-form assignment from the author as assignor to the producer as assignee, and a mortgage of all the producer's right, title, and interest in the photoplay including the literary property by the producer to the distributor.

Another document ordinarily prepared is a laboratory pledgeholder's agreement. This document is executed by the producer, the distributor, the laboratory that will be doing the so-called "front end work" (the preparation of the negative or preprint materials), and the laboratory that will do the release printing from the negative materials. The agreement ordinarily provides that the laboratory is a pledgeholder for the distributor and is holding the materials for the distributor's disposal. Unless the distributor otherwise specifies in writing, the producer has access to the materials for production purposes. However, if the distri-

85

butor notifies the laboratory, the agreement provides that the laboratory is required to deliver the materials to the distributor.

One should be conscious of the fact that if a film is going to be produced overseas, there are problems involved in obtaining security documentation. In the United Kingdom, for instance, there is a substantial charge for recording a lien. Because the charge is so substantial, many companies do not bother recording liens in connection with United Kingdom productions. In France and Italy, there is a central cinematographic registry, and any document relating to the ownership of rights in the photoplay is supposed to be noted with this registry. The registration presumably protects the party making the registration against subsequent conflicting assignments to third parties and creates what is in essence a security interest. Obviously, local counsel must be retained in connection with such documentation. Even more so than in the U.S., litigation overseas, if necessary, is expensive, hazardous in the extreme, and highly time-consuming.

As already mentioned, some P-Ds give the distributor the right to foreclose in the absence of a default if the distributor does not recoup the production costs, with interest, within a stated period of time. This concept enables a distributor to buy the film at its unrecouped cost at a foreclosure sale, and thereafter own it outright free of any obligation to account to the producer. If the unrecouped amount is small, the producer could conceivably bid for the film at the sale.

If there is a foreclosure, whether or not because of the producer's breach, the producer will not want to be responsible for any deficiency if the foreclosure sale does not bring enough money to reimburse the distributor for production costs. Distributors usually agree to look only to the picture in any foreclosure proceeding and not to the producer's other assets. This kind of mortgage is sometimes called a dry mortgage, as was previously pointed out.

It is interesting to note that although all of the security documentation in connection with a motion picture is customarily executed and recorded, one rarely hears of any lawsuits testing the sufficiency of the security documentation. In other words, production companies do not ordinarily go bankrupt or become insolvent in the middle of the production of the photoplay, and distributors do not ordinarily institute a lawsuit against the producer in the middle of the production of a film to determine rights and attempt to foreclose as part of the litigation. As a matter of fact, foreclosure proceedings, if a film does not recoup its production costs, are rare.

If a distributor does not want to litigate because of the inherent costs and dangers of litigation, no matter what the distributor's contractual rights, what can the distributor do if it thinks the producer is not fulfilling his obligations, but the distributor can not prove a breach by the producer? Even if the producer is fulfilling his contractual obligations, what contractual remedy can the distributor impose upon the producer to make sure that the production does not exceed the budget or run behind the shooting schedule?

Under certain circumstances, as pointed out, the distributor will have the right to take over the actual production of the photoplay.

In calculating whether or not the cost of production will exceed the final budget by a given percentage, most production accountants will furnish to the distributor a figure called *cost to complete*—an estimate of how much money will be required to complete the production of the photoplay. As part of the distributor's financial controls, the distributor will receive a weekly cost statement indicating costs incurred during the week, as well as current cumulative costs for producing the photoplay. In addition, the distributor will be furnished with a cost to complete schedule and a daily production sheet indicating exactly what scenes were photographed on each day, which members of the cast were utilized, the number of extras, etc. This sheet along with the approved shooting schedule can give a very close idea of how the production is faring.

In the event the distributor actually takes over production of the photoplay, the agreements provide that the producer assign to the distributor all of the contracts and agreements with production personnel, and the distributor will continue with the cost of production of the photoplay. In this case, the distributor solely will disburse production funds and the producer no longer can sign checks in payment for the production.

Another contract provision sometimes used to induce the producer to control the cost of producing the photoplay is a clause stating that in the event the cost of production exceeds the final budget, the producer's share of net receipts are decreased and the distributor's share increased by a stated formula—sometimes one percentage point for each unit of 1% of ½% (or fraction thereof) that the cost of production exceeds the final budget. Consequently, if the final budget is $3 million and each unit is 1% of the final budget, each percentage point would be $30,000.

This formula does not accomplish its purpose if the final budget of the photoplay is either extremely large or extremely small. For instance, if the budget of the photoplay is $1 million, each unit would only be $10,000 and the producer would be in a precarious position, and penalized for even slight increases over budget. On the other hand, if the final budget of the photoplay were $10 million or more, each unit would be $100,000, and this would unfairly favor the producer, since net receipts to a producer would not be reduced sufficiently to penalize him. Sometimes the penalty for overbudget cost is expressed as a percentage but with an upper limit such as $50,000 for each percentage point. This protects a distributor of a high-budget film. In assessing this provision, a producer will argue that the final budget should include a contingency sum. The contingency sum is expressed as a percentage of the budget and is supposed to cover contingencies which are not planned for in the budgeting, such as Acts of God, and unforeseen circumstances which the producer cannot control. Even the amount of the contingency may be negotiated. Ordinarily, the contingency is 10% of the budget for location shooting, where there are more possibilities for unforeseen events, and possibly 5% to 10% for shooting at a studio. Presumably, it is possible that if there are special or unique difficulties in producing the film, the contingency should be larger that 10%. If there are no difficulties involved, the contingency might be less. The contingency fund is not supposed to be used for overbudget costs due to the producer's negligence. The producer will try to treat the contingency sum as a part of the budget for purposes of computing any penalty. The producer will also try to exclude *force majeure* items, as well as other items that could not reasonably have been forseen by the producer, such as costs due to labor increases occurring during the term of the production of the photoplay and costs incurred by default or delay of the distributor.

Because of these penalty clauses, it is very important for the producer to make sure that the budget contains a margin of error. Some producers try to pad a budget so that it will be relatively easy to bring the picture within the budget. In the film business, producers are given a good deal of credit if they bring films in on, or under budget. Whether or not those films should, in fact, have been budgeted for less initially is irrelevent. On the other hand, if the producer budgets the film too high, the distributor may not agree to finance the film. Just as producers sometimes submit artificially high budgets, distributors sometimes try to reduce the budget to an artificially low level. This may be done for many reasons. For public relations purposes, it may be better for the distributor to announce that the picture is budgeted at $1 million, even though the distributor may know that it is possible that the picture will cost $200,000 or $300,000 more than that. Conceivably (but not honestly), this may happen if there is third party financing, so that a financier will be persuaded to advance funds. There is a great temptation for the producer to accept, if necessary, any figure, whether or not reasonable, to which the distributor reduces the budget, for the producer will have spent months assembling the package and getting ready to produce the photoplay, and he will want to be paid his production fee. Since such a small number of photoplays ever show net receipts, the producer probably will not be too concerned about losing net receipts if the producer is overbudget. Therefore, if the film is over the budget, he will take the risk that his profit participation may be reduced because of a penalty provision.

As a matter of fact, the producer may be one of the persons least responsible for the fact that the photoplay is exceeding the budget; the persons more responsible would include the director and stars. The director is the person primarily responsible for shooting the photoplay, and if he insists upon retaking a scene 20 times, and shooting exorbitant amounts of footage, or if an actor continually flubs lines and requires retakes, obviously the costs will soar. Sometimes the producer may find it very difficult to control the director. No matter how well the producer has planned the production of the photoplay, a wasteful director or a recalcitrant cast member can usually defeat the producer's purposes.

Probably the main difficulty with the concept of adjustments of profits is that for the provision to be effective at all, there must be profits. If there are no profits, it of course makes no difference what the producer does to increase to the cost of production exceeding the budget, for he cannot have taken away from him what he does not have. Conversely, if there are profits, no matter how much the cost of production has exceeded the final budget, the producer will have made money for the distributor, who will have received distribution fees and will have recouped all distribution expenses and the cost of production with interest. In that event, the distributor will want more than anything else to keep the producer's good will, for the producer may want to be involved in another film produced by the distributor. To start penalizing the producer by adjusting profits on a profitable picture is hardly the way to go about doing this. For this reason, it is very rare that distribution companies enforce an adjustment of profits clause in an agreement. More likely, the clause is used as a bargaining tool so that if a picture goes over the budget, the distributor will waive the provision, and in so doing will hope to get the producer to do another picture for the distributor or receive some other concession.

Some companies have recently been experimenting with variations on the adjustment of profits provisions. What they may do is to add a percentage of the amount that the cost of production exceeds the final budget to the cost of production, and this artificial sum is then recouped by the distributor before there are profits to be shared. In other words, the producer's share of net receipts would be deferred until the artificial sum is recouped, which means the overbudget costs are doubled for the purpose of recoupment. The advantage of this provision is that it is somewhat self-executing. It is also more palatable since there is a definite relation between the amount of the penalty and the overbudget cost and there is no reduction of the percentage of the producer's share of net receipts, only a postponement of when he receives them.

In these days of studio economies and tight monies, distributors want to be doubly sure that a picture that is budgeted for a specific sum does not cost the distributor substantially more. More and more, distributors are undertaking to finance the film only up to the approved budget and are insisting that producers supply

90

completion money, that is, money utilized to complete the cost of production of the photoplay if the cost of production exceeds the final budget. The completion money can take various forms. Sometimes the producer will be asked to defer a portion of his fee and that portion is utilized as completion money. In other words, if the producer's fee is $100,000, and the producer defers $50,000 of that amount, then if the photoplay is budgeted at $1 million, the first $50,000 spent over that amount is taken from the producer's fee. If the producer has previously made a picture for the distributor, and the distributor is paying net receipts to the producer for the prior film, then there may be a provision that some of this money due be withheld and applied as completion money for the latter picture.

Completion Guarantor

In the event that completion money is provided for, it is customary for the person advancing the completion money to recoup the sums advanced, if any, in second position; that is, immediately after the distributor. In other words, the distributor will first be repaid all of its production advances with interest and then the person advancing the completion money will recoup that amount of money with interest. Note that completion money is an advance which usually is repaid only from the proceeds of the film. If the completion money is a loan, the producer alone is responsible for repayment.

Sometimes a distributor will not be willing to accept completion money from deferred sums because this completion money almost always has a ceiling on it. In other words, a producer may be willing to defer $50,000 of the producer's fee, but if the cost of the production exceeds the final approved budget by more that $50,000, someone must still finance the excess. The best protection for a distributor is to find a company or person who will advance completion money to complete the production of the photoplay, no matter how much the cost of production exceeds the final budget. This type of person is called a *completion guarantor*. The completion bond business is very risky, since a runaway production creates an open-end obligation on the part of the completion guarantor company. Consequently, there are only a handful of companies in the U.S. and Great Britain that are in

91

the business of advancing completion money. It is sometimes difficult to assess the financial stability of these companies, since some of them are limited partnerships and others are closely held corporations; and it is impossible to find out whether or not a particular company could afford to pay a substantial loss, since they do not usually publish financial information. The best protection is to ascertain how long the company has been in business and how it handles claims.

Most usually the completion guarantor will charge a fee based upon a percentage of the final budget which fee is paid when the completion bond is executed. Occasionally, completion guarantors will insist upon a percentage of the net receipts from the film, as well. The fee, when based on the final budget, is sometimes also based upon the contingency sum, but is not based on contingent payments such as deferments or profit participations. This fee is almost always at least 5%; thus, the completion guarantor company may receive a large fee, but may never have to advance money, if the film is within the budget. So there are advantages to equal the risks of the business. Sometimes, if the completion guarantor is not called upon to advance money, a portion of the fee is rebated to the producer. This rebate is an inducement to the producer to bring the film in on budget. If the distributor is financing the cost of production of the photoplay, the distributor should see to it that if the producer receives a rebate, that rebate is turned over to the distributor.

Sophisticated completion guarantors will first look at all of the production agreements very carefully and will then scrupulously examine the final budget. A completion guarantor is somewhat in the same position as the producer; that is, the more the budget has margins for error, the less likely it will be that the completion guarantor will have to advance monies. Sometimes the guarantor, as a condition of furnishing a bond, will insist that the budget be increased.

The completion guarantor will also check the shooting schedule, the shooting locations, the insurance, and every other element of the production. If there are unusual or extreme risks, the fee may be higher. Some completion companies will hesitate to write a completion bond for a film to be shot in a locale with which they are not familiar. One English company engaged in this business has

92

not, to our knowledge, written any completion bonds in the U.S., mainly because they do not have production personnel they can rely on to supervise productions here.

From the distributor's point of view, what the completion guarantor agrees to do is to assure finances so that the distributor is furnished a completed photoplay with the various elements approved by the distributor, including the script, the cast, and the director. If the producer delivers the photoplay to the distributor and the completion guarantor avoids its obligation to advance overbudget cost by causing the producer to eliminate 20 pages of the script, that is not what the distributor has bargained for. Ordinarily, the guarantor will have a representative on the set to watch and review the progress of the production. The guarantor will usually receive the same production reports as the distributor, from the producer, and the guarantor will be assigned the distributor's rights to take over production of the film or obtain its own takeover right if the distributor has no rights of takeover. Whether or not the guarantor would obtain the right under certain circumstances to replace talent or a director of the film, if the film is over the budget, is a matter for negotiation.

Ordinarily, the guarantor will insist on co-signing all production checks, thus giving the guarantor some financial control over expenditures. As a practical matter, the completion guarantor will be as reluctant to take over production of the photoplay as the distributor, and will, therefore, try to make economies in the production by utilizing the threat of a takeover to achieve results. In lieu of completing and delivering the picture, a guarantor may take the alternative rights of terminating the production and repaying the expended or incurred portion of the cost of production to the distributor. Sometimes it may be cheaper for a completion guarantor to terminate rather than complete, but a distributor may insist on the completion of the film unless death or disability of a cast member or director makes it impossible.

The guarantor will also want to make sure that its own responsibility does not begin until the contingency fund has been spent. It will, therefore, want to make sure that a reasonable contingency fund is provided depending on where the film will be photographed—whether on location or at a studio.

A guarantor may not look only to the gross receipts of the film

93

for recoupment, but may want a lien or security interest in the film, subject to the distributor's lien, to insure against the insolvency of the producer or distributor or third party claims against the film. Whether the guarantor can insist on such a security interest depends upon who the distributor is and the guarantor's bargaining position.

It is very important for the distributor to know how much control the guarantor intends to exercise during the production of the photoplay. If the guarantor is likely to start acting like the producer of the film, it is possible for the guarantor and the producer to get into arguments and extended fights so that the whole production suffers.

Although the guarantee business is an extremely risky one, it can be very profitable. It is possible that the guarantor will get a fee and never have to advance any money. Presumably, the guarantor, in assessing whether or not to become a completion guarantor, will make some subjective judgment as to the quality of the photoplay, the reputation of the producer, and other intangibles, including the experience of the director and the cast, in addition to the objective examination of the budget, etc., discussed previously. The guarantor must believe that the film has a reasonable chance to succeed, for it is not likely to advance monies that it will probably not get back.

In the event there is a completion guarantor, or other completion money, the producer may argue that there should be no adjustment of profit or other penalty to the producer for going over the budget, since the provision for completion money sufficiently protects the distributor without the necessity of penalizing the producer. However, from the distributor's point of view, to the extent that the guarantor must recoup money, the distributor's share of the profits will be deferred. There are, or at least used to be, private financiers in the completion bond business who do not bother with sophisticated reviews or production documents; nor do they bother to have representatives on the set. They will probably seek either a substantially larger fee or a larger percentage of the profits.

In computing recoupment of a guarantor's advance, the guarantor will ordinarily accept the definition of gross receipts, distribution fees, and distribution expenses contained in the P-D be-

94

tween the producer and the distributor. However, it is conceivable that a guarantor might argue that a distributor should reduce its fee, distribution fees, or interest charges, or make some other concessions in order to obtain an agreement for the completion money. Again, the resolution of the difference will depend upon the bargaining power of the parties. If the completion guarantor is guaranteed repayment of any monies advanced from some source other than gross receipts derived from the distribution of the photoplay (and this is most unusual), then the guarantor is merely another form of lender, and is not a completion guarantor as the term is commonly used.

Methods of Distribution

In almost every P-D, the distributor retains the sole and exclusive right to distribute the photoplay by any and all media worldwide (or these days, throughout the universe) in perpetuity. Generally, there is no question but that the distributor obtains these rights, especially if the distributor has fully financed the production of the photoplay.

Some producers will try to write into the P-D some sort of buyout formula effective after a given number of years. These formulas are designed to establish the producer's interest in the film, since the producer obtains the right to repurchase the film from the distributor. Usually, the formula is expressed in such a way that it would be financially unprofitable for the producer to exercise such rights. Whether or not a particular distribution company will agree to accept such a formula again will depend upon the relative bargaining power of the parties and the particular company involved.

In the past, some well-known talent has had sufficient bargaining power to own all rights in a film and has leased the rights to the financier-distributor for a term of years. At the end of the given number of years, all rights in the film reverted to the talent. At the present moment, it is not clear whether any talent still has that kind of bargaining position. Most financier-distributors will fiercely resist a license concept for a limited term.

The distributor's rights to distribute by any method or media means not only distribution in theatres, on television, or in nontheatrical locations, but also means distribution by new media such as cassettes, cartridges, community antenna television, and any media yet to be invented. Although a distributor may be experienced in distributing theatrically and non-theatrically, and may have a television sales department experienced in making network and syndication sales, a producer may well ask whether or not a particular distributor has the expertise to distribute in some new media in which no standards have been established.

There are a number of new developments, such as cassettes, closed circuit television in hotels, etc., and pay television systems interconnected by cables to form a countrywide system of connections, which may serve to revolutionize the motion picture industry. To the extent that these elements either diminish or increase the risk of financing the production of motion pictures, or change in some way the speed of the distributor's recoupment, bargaining guidelines between the producer and distributor will also change. For instance, if a motion picture distributor can make a deal with a series of interconnected pay television cable systems to have a motion picture exhibited before an audience of ten or twenty million people in one night, then the payment from the community antenna system for just one viewing might equal or exceed the cost of production of the film. Under such circumstances the risk would be taken out of motion picture financing, the distributor's expertise and sales force would have hardly any relevance, and the return on the investment to produce the film would be guaranteed.

The likelihood of the exhibition of motion pictures by a satellite or tape cartridge also opens new vistas from the point of view of the distributor. Such new developments mean that the distributor's traditional expertise may be less important in the new markets that result.

A similar analogy may be found in the music publishing business. In the old days, almost all music sold as sheet music, piano copies, or orchestrations. That period was the day of the song-plugger, and the music publishers were active in promoting new compositions and seeing to it that the catalog was played. The music publisher used his experience and expertise to devise new editions and new versions of the music.

With the development of the record industry, records became the important medium for promoting music, and music today is

96

promoted by record companies and the acts themselves. The role of the music publishers as a force of promotion of music is now diminished. Since the role of the music publisher as promoter for the music was decreased, the recording artists, many of them also writers, realized that they, too, could share in the royalties derived from publishing, and many of them formed their own publishing companies. The function of the publishing company is now to finance acquisition of catalogs and to a large extent finance up-and-coming songwriters in return for the publishing rights to compositions written. This may be the role of major motion picture distribution companies if patterns of distribution change, although it is still too early to tell.

The difficulty with film production is that the best chance to make money is in distribution, but to get the distribution, the majors had to finance productions. Even though there is a greater public acceptance of low-budget films and many smaller distribution companies are entering the field, it is still a fact that motion pictures usually cost at least several hundred thousands of dollars, and raising the money to produce a motion picture without a distributor is not easy. Some of the ways this can be done are enumerated in later chapters of this book.

The smaller distributors will find it more difficult to find films of public appeal to distribute unless they finance the production or pay advances for completed films. Can a small independent distributor successfully distribute pictures? As of this date, there is no doubt that if one seeks a big, commercial release, a major distributor is a must. The major distributor has the sales force, the sales offices in major cities, the personal contacts with the theatres, and the know-how to see to it that a large-scale motion picture can be released successfully all over the country.

With a small art house type picture, an independent producer may be able to achieve very satisfactory results distributing primarily in big cities, which provide the bulk of film revenues. This pattern of distribution skims the cream off the top of the market since the cost of prints to theatres in a small town may be more than the revenue derived. The small distributors say that a large sales force and large amounts of advertising are unnecessary. They say that more than ever before, successful pictures depend upon a combination of good critical reviews and word of mouth. Some pictures may get poor critical reviews but are so pitched to the family audience that the word of mouth can contribute to its success whether the critics like it or dislike it. Other pictures may receive no critical response but still do tremendous business because of word of mouth or other reasons. One or two pictures that opened in New York during a newspaper strike received no newspaper reviews at all, and although the traditional means of advertising was gone, the pictures did tremendous business because of the favorable responses of the people who had seen them.

It is claimed that one of the difficult parts of the distribution business is expanding a small, art-house big city distribution into a general commercial distribution. In the present boom or bust state of the business, a picture usually does either a relatively large amount of business, or none at all. It has been said that if a picture is bad, it does not matter how many salesmen try to sell it, and if it is good, no salesmen are needed because the film sells itself. This, too, of course, is somewhat of an oversimplification. In fact, most pictures must be sold, and a good picture, if it is sold properly, will do better. A bad picture, if it is properly sold, should at least do some business.

Since, usually, only the major distributors finance production, from the point of view of negotiating a P-D, it is a foregone conclusion that if the distributor is going to put up all the money, it will want to have complete and total distribution rights. It may be argued that the distributor has great expertise in distributing theatrically, but perhaps someone else should distribute in some other media. This argument may have some validity, but it has nothing to do with the reality of present day negotiations with major film distributors in the motion picture business. This would, in effect, be asking the distributor to bid for the right to distribute a picture it has financed.

Most P-Ds have pages devoted to the proposition that the distributor can distribute the picture any way it wishes, free from any complaint by the producer. The distributor typically has the broadest possible discretion and latitude, and the exercise of the distributor's judgment is usually valid and binding. Usually a distributor will agree to release the picture but will not usually guarantee the type or pattern of release. If it does release the film, it may release it on any terms it wishes.

98

What should or can a producer do to modify the broad language in the P-D, which gives the distributor such complete freedom in distributing the photoplay? Some attorneys for producers will insist upon adding language to the effect that the distributor will exercise good faith in distributing the photoplay. The efficacy of the language is questionable, since it would appear doubtful that any distributor will admit to distributing in bad faith. Anyway, the courts would construe the agreement as obligating the parties to act in good faith.

Some producers will try to add a clause to the effect that the distributor will exercise reasonable business judgment in the distribution. Again, presumably, a distributor can usually justify from a business point of view any decision it makes. Even so, the distributor's attorneys will probably more strongly resist an attempt to insert language such as "reasonable business judgment" than "good faith." This is because various distribution companies from time to time will run into financial problems, and these problems may cause the distributor to release the picture so as to generate money quickly. To effect the quick return of income, the distributor may make unwarranted sacrifices, such as a television sale somewhat earlier than it should be, or distribution of the photoplay to exhibitors on a different release pattern than would have been the case had the distributor the financial stability to sustain itself while the photoplay was in distribution. It is possible that a producer would not get a fair shake as a result of this kind of distribution arrangement. Is this a failure to exercise reasonable business judgment? The distributor will not want to permit having its books and records examined to determine whether each engagement was the best one obtainable or whether the television sale might have been better or have been made at some future time. Almost everyone can tell you what you should have done, but would the producer have had the expertise to tell the distributor what to do before the distributor did it?

There are, of course, well-known instances of photoplays that were, in fact, incorrectly distributed. Some errant distributors will even admit this. There have been times for example when a distributor thought it had a general release picture which later turned out to be a high-quality art house picture. The film might have grossed more playing in a few selected theatres for a long period of time to build up the word of mouth. Instead, the picture was exhibited simultaneously in a large number of theatres for a limited period of time. Consequently, the film had completed its distribution before people realized how good it was. It sometimes happens that the distributor will not know the quality of the picture it has. There have been occasions when a film has been tossed on the market with scant ceremony, only to receive glowing critical reviews.

Another approach in negotiating the P-D is to obligate the distributor to use its best efforts in distributing the photoplay. Again, there is a question as to what constitutes "best efforts," and how to determine whether or not a distributor is in fact using its best efforts. Generally, this language is difficult to obtain since it does in fact imply a standard of conduct. Best efforts might mean distributing a film to the detriment of another film of the distributor. Best efforts to maximize gross receipts might mean spending unnecessary advertising or print dollars which after recoupment might mean fewer net receipts. Maximizing net receipts might make the distributor reluctant to spend advertising dollars which might otherwise be spent. All of these requests for a contractual generalized standard of conduct for distribution are calculated to give the producer a better litigating position in the event of a lawsuit. There is really no way to set up a specific objective standard for judging distribution. Either someone is distributing properly, or he is not. Either someone is using good faith, or he is not. From the distributor's point of view, good faith in the distribution of the photoplay should be evidenced by the fact that the distributor has paid all of the costs of financing it and would have powerful inducement to at least recoup its investment. The distributor will feel that the producer, although he may know something about producing, will know nothing about distributing the photoplay.

The clauses just mentioned would serve to give the producer a bargaining position in the event of a lawsuit by adding language imposing some general obligations on the distributor. The question may be asked as to whether any contractual obligations can be imposed on the distributor to affirmatively undertake specific obligations in connection with distribution.

Sometimes all a distributor will agree to do is to give a photoplay a theatrical release. The producer wants a theatrical release to be sure that the distributor does not merely license the photoplay to television. What does the term *theatrical release* mean? Does it mean merely a release in one theatre, or does it mean a general release in many theatres? A producer might insist that the film be released in first run theatres in certain key cities within a stated period of time.

Ordinarily, unless the film is created specifically for television, the distributor will agree to give it a theatrical release in the U.S., but will usually not specify the type of release to be given.

Additionally, the producer may request that the agreement provide that the distributor itself distribute the photoplay theatrically in the U.S., and possibly in major foreign territories if the distributor has an organization there. As will be seen later, certain non-major distributors do not themselves distribute in all areas of the U.S., but utilize licensees called *states righters* to handle subdistribution for them in those areas where they do not distribute. The producer argues that he picked a certain distributor to distribute for him, and that distributor should itself distribute. The distributor might want to be able to assign certain distribution rights such as non-theatrical rights to a subdistributor, or assign the entire agreement to a corporation into which the distributor may be merged. If a producer wants to make certain that a particular distributor will in fact itself distribute, the agreement could provide that the first general release of the picture be handled by the distributor.

Certain distributors have their own organizations overseas to handle foreign distribution. Some of these organizations own their theatres and, typically, the film will play in those theatres. All of the safeguards to insure arms-length dealing between distributors and their own theatres would apply overseas as well as in the U.S. The distributor should be contractually obligated to make an arms-length deal with its theatre, and to receive the same terms from its theatre that a third party would get if that party licensed a picture into the distributor's theatre. As noted, some distributors include, as a supplement to the P-D, the terms of the agreements that it will make with its theatres.

The producer will also want to make sure that the picture is distributed in all parts of the world, and should request that the

101

picture not be licensed on an outright sale basis for a flat fixed sum in certain major territories such as Canada, France, the United Kingdom, Germany, Australia, Japan, Spain, and Italy.

Ordinarily, a distributor will agree that the picture will not be sold outright in the major territories of the world. If the distributor has its own subsidiaries or affiliated companies in these territories, it usually agrees that these companies will handle the distribution.

It is customary, however, for some of the minor territories to be sold on an outright basis. It is usually difficult to remit monies from these smaller territories and to insure proper accountings, even if remittances can be made on a regular basis. The major distributors will customarily make outright sales in some of the minor territories, where it is not worth their while to keep sales offices.

A producer may want to provide in the agreement that if certain stated major territories are not licensed within a given period of time, the producer can make a deal with subdistributors in these territories. In that event, the distributor would either match the deal and distribute in the territory, or lose the territory. In the latter case the producer's subdistributors would account to the distributor. For instance, the agreement might provide that if the territory of France were not sold for a three-year period, the producer could find a subdistributor for the territory and present the proposed deal to the distributor. The distributor would then have to accept the deal with the subdistributor, or lose the territory. Usually, the distributor would have to accept the deal only if the distributor would not be obligated to advance any sums to pay for prints or advertising. The distributor would take a reduced distribution fee for only administering the deal.

Although on paper this kind of propositon may sound good from a producer's point of view, in actuality, if the picture can be distributed in a territory on any kind of economic basis, the distributor will undoubtedly do so or arrange for subdistribution. If the distributor does not choose to distribute in a territory and has not been able to license the film to a subdistributor in a territory, there is small hope that the producer will be able to come up with a deal. Most distributors are not unwilling to insert this sort of provision in a P-D, for they believe that they will

102

undoubtedly be able to distribute or license the distribution of the major markets with any picture that they bother financing.

Opinions vary as to the kind of an agreement a distributor should make with subdistributors for a particular territory. If the distributor tries to obtain a large cash advance from a subdistributor, the subdistributor paying the advance will charge and retain a larger distribution fee because the payment of the advance increases the risk of obtaining a profit on the film. A distributor obtaining a large cash advance does not usually expect any overages after the subdistributor has deducted and retained its fee and expenses, and recouped the advance from gross receipts. If the distributor wants to go on a straight distribution arrangement, there is sometimes difficulty because of government regulations in remitting money from the territory. Some independent distributors will do all of their licensing of films through one subdistributor. In this kind of an arrangement, the independent distributor has the advantage of usually employing supervisory personnel, and will have day-to-day supervision over the kind of distribution effected by the subdistributor.

A producer attempting to regulate distribution expenses tries to insert in the contract a ceiling on the amounts a distributor can spend for prints and advertising of a film. Some distribution companies say they will not manufacture more than a given number of prints, or spend more than a stated amount for advertising without the producer's consent, but these amounts are generally so high that in all likelihood they will never be reached.

Presumably, the most important thing for a producer is to pick the right kind of distributor for the particular picture. As a practical matter, most disputes with distributors after the picture is released concern the distributor's accounting deductions and bookkeeping arrangements. Any argument over sales policy is usually just an excuse upon which the producer's attorney will rely to exact concessions or effect a settlement. Usually, a dispute will arise only over successful pictures—no one audits a flop. It is very difficult to support the argument that the distributor could have achieved even higher grosses with a successful movie.

Accounting Procedures

A producer is concerned about when he gets his money, and

103

this is why the accounting provisions of the agreement should be examined with some care. Most P-Ds provide for accountings either monthly or quarterly on an annual basis for a stated number of years, thereafter semi-annually, and then annually. Accountings are usually rendered either 45 or 60 days after the end of each accounting period. The fewer accountings there are, and the longer the distributor has to render the accounting after the close of an accounting period, the more the producer loses, as the producer cannot earn interest on money he has not received; however, interest will be charged by the distributor on the unrecouped cost of production during that period. It is to the producer's advantage to receive accountings as frequently as possible during the period of time that the film is being continuously distributed, and it is also well for the producer to provide that if any substantial amounts (in a stated amount) of income are received, they must be reported promptly (within a stated period).

For instance, if a photoplay has been released theatrically and the agreement provides that accounting statements are rendered yearly after the first five years of release, and the photoplay is sold to television six years after release, the distributor could receive the television income (which might be substantial) and be under no obligation to report any of it to the producer for a year. This situation is technically possible under the language used in many P-Ds.

Most agreements provide that statements will be rendered either on a billings basis or a collections basis. Obviously, a billings basis ✗ is more favorable to the producer because the producer will get credit for amounts billed before they are collected. If the amounts are not collected, the statement will be subsequently adjusted, but in the meantime the producer will have had the benefit of the use of the money and at least interest will not be running on the money. If the accounting is on a collections basis, the producer will get reports based only on the money that the distributor has, in fact, collected. If the accounting statements provide that the method of accounting can be changed, the producer could rightly insist that any change be permitted only if the change is made for all of the pictures for which the distributor is rendering accountings.

Some agreements will provide that the distributor does not have

104

*billed by distrib
against sales offices?

to render an accounting to the producer if the amount due on any accounting period does not exceed a stated sum, such as $5,000. The producer may argue that if any money is due him, he should get it. A distributor will not want to be obligated to render accounting statements if the picture is pretty much out of release and the cost of the film is totally unrecouped. The compromise is to provide that so long as the cost of the picture is unrecouped, the distributor does not have to render accounting statements unless the amount of gross receipts reported exceeds $5,000 in any particular period.

Most agreements will provide that foreign receipts are accounted for in the currency received by the distributor. The distributor will ordinarily use reasonable efforts to convert receipts into U.S. dollars at whatever rate of exchange it can obtain. Ordinarily, the distributor will provide contractually that it is not liable for any errors of judgment, if it makes a bona fide effort to convert to dollars.

In the event that a distributor cannot receive money from a foreign country because the currency regulations of that country provide that the sums are frozen there (this is referred to as *blocked currency*), the agreement will generally provide that the producer can require the distributor to deposit the money in an account of the producer in the foreign country. In some cases, the foreign currency can be used for purchases in the foreign country, though the money cannot be exported. For instance, some well-known authors have taken trips to the Soviet Union and spent large sums of money there because they cannot export money due them from the Russian government. If there is blocked currency, and the producer does not request that the money be deposited to his account in the foreign country, it is not unreasonable to request that if the currency becomes unblocked, then it is unblocked on a first in-first out basis. In other words, the monies blocked earliest would be released earliest.

Most agreements try to impose some sort of artificial time limitation on the right to audit. For instance, they will provide that a statement is binding unless objected to within a stated period of time, and unless a lawsuit is started within a stated period of time from the date of the objection. The agreement will probably also provide that audits can only be held a limited

105

number of times during a stated time period, can continue for a limited period, and can only cover a stipulated period of accounting statements rendered prior to the audit. The agreement may possibly provide that the producer can only make one audit a year, can audit any period commencing two years prior to the date the inspection commences, and that the inspection cannot continue for more than 30 consecutive days. The reason for these restrictions, the distributor says, is to simplify the distributor's bookkeeping and to avoid harassment. The distributor will not want to maintain its records for a long and indefinite period of time, nor will it want the producer's accountants disrupting routine and turning its records inside out.

On the other hand, a producer wants unlimited audit rights. Usually, the time periods fixed are negotiable. The contractual provision for time limitations may put the producer in the position of having to enforce his rights by formally objecting to every statement and sending accountants in to audit. There are some accouting firms that are experienced in motion picture accounting and auditing, and these firms can usually unearth anything a distributor can do which may conceivably be improper under the terms of the agreement.

One favorite subject of an audit is the question of allocations. One example of the problem occurs when a distributor licenses a picture as part of a double feature with another picture of the distributor. If the distributor owns one picture outright, but has the other picture on a net receipts arrangement, the temptation would be to allocate a larger portion of receipts to the picture which is owned outright and thus to discriminate against the picture in which a portion of the net receipts must be paid to the producer. The same is true with television syndication. It is not uncommon for several pictures to be sold as a group to a television station. To avoid anti-trust claims, the distributor will allow a station to license all or a portion of the pictures in the package. Some distributors insist that the purchase price of each picture in the package be negotiated separately. If the price is not negotiated separately, the fee must be allocated to each film in the package.

Many television networks and stations will want to make the allocation themselves for their own accounting purposes since the cost of a film should bear some relationship to the advertising dollars that can be earned for selling time. To that extent, distributors will have nothing to do with the allocation. Often, however, the distributor must make an allocation. Television syndicators sometimes assign letter values to each picture in a package. For instance, an AA picture may be worth twice as much as an A, and an A may be worth 50% more than a B, and so on. These allocations are at best rough estimates, and sometimes a producer will feel rightly that the allocation to his picture is less than it should be. However, a distributor in allocating pictures must think of more than just the picture's theatrical gross receipts. The market for pictures on television differs from the market for pictures theatrically. Some pictures are too risqué to play on television at all; others cannot be shown on prime time. Some famous foreign pictures, dubbed into English, do not sell well on television, nor do pictures in black and white.

Under the usual television deal, pictures are sold to television well in advance of the time that they will be exhibited on the station, and the money is usually payable to the distributor in installments. Assuming that the total license fee has been apportioned to each film in a package, the question still remains as to how to allocate a portion of each installment payment to each individual photoplay. One method is to allocate the money as it is paid to the distributor in the order that each picture is used or made available for release on television. Another method would be to allocate each payment when received *pro rata* among all of the pictures. This allocation is generally not regulated by contract, but rather by accounting practice, and reasonable accountants can and do differ on what is proper allocation.

The same sort of allocation problem will arise when a number of pictures are licensed to a foreign market either on an outright sale basis or for a minimum guarantee against a percentage of the gross receipts.

Another problem arises with respect to whether a given tax is deductible from gross receipts. Somes taxes are clearly based upon the gross receipts of a film or the remittance of money and should be deductible as distribution expenses. Some taxes are not so clearly categorized, however, and may be based on a foreign subsidiary's earnings, and there may be a problem as to whether such taxes are deductible as distributor's expenses.

The allocation of advertising can also create disputes. Sometimes a company will run ads for a number of films. Should the cost of the ads be prorated in proportion to the amount of space devoted to each picture, to the theatrical gross receipts derived by the picture, or should some other standard be utilized? If a promotional trailer, which will promote a number of the distributor's motion pictures, is manufactured, the same allocation problems occur. There is no problem, to the extent that the work involved can be directly attributable to an individual picture, but some costs are generally common to all of the pictures.

A producer must weigh the possible benefits from an audit against its cost. Some producers will try to provide in the agreement that if the actual amount found to be due the producer, as a result of an audit, varies from the amount originally reported by the distributor by more than a specified percentage or dollar amount, the distributor will pay for the cost of the producer's audit. This hardly meets with any favor from distributors, but the argument is that a distributor should reimburse the producer if errors in accounting are discovered, whether deliberate or inadvertent.

One key concern of most distributors is that the producer has a right to audit only the books applicable to the producer's film and not the other photoplays of the distributor. This, of course, will make it more difficult for a producer to check allocations, or to check how the photoplay was distributed. It would be interesting for a producer to know that a certain picture which grossed X dollars had 5,000 playdates, while the producer's own photoplay, which grossed Y dollars, had only 3,000 playdates. It would also be interesting for a producer to check the relative sums of advertising spent and the number of prints ordered for different movies. Of course, the distributor's answer to all of this is that other movies distributed by the distributor are none of the producer's business, and disclosure of facts about other movies would violate the confidential relationship between the distributor and its other producers. This argument usually prevails.

If a particular distribution or exhibition agreement makes reference to more than one photoplay, most distributors will allow the producer to inspect the particular agreement, which of course indicates the allocation made. However, the distributor will not ordinarily disclose underlying information with respect to the agreements.

At the end of the audit, the producer's accountants and the distributor's accounting department will get together and try to resolve their differences. Usually, they are able to do so. However, sometimes they cannot and litigation results. By and large, this kind of litigation rarely turns upon the contractual language. It is more usually decided upon accounting concepts and procedures. There is very little that a distributor can do to cover all the situations that may arise and protect itself against this kind of litigation.

The other items in audits which can create a big problem are miscellaneous expense items. For instance, if a company's executives make a trip, can the trip be charged to the photoplay? If the executives see two or three pictures, how are the costs broken down?

Note that the auditor's job is to establish that the amount of money received was correctly reported as gross receipts, and that any deductions from those gross receipts were proper. It is not an auditor's role to ask whether or not more gross receipts should have been obtained, for he would not be acting as an accountant; rather he would be criticizing the sales policies of the distributor.

Ordinarily, the distributor will allow the accountants to examine only home office records and will not permit them to examine records of subdistributors in other territories, or even records in the distributor's exchanges (those regional offices where the films are licensed to exhibitors). Most of the exchange office records are duplicated in the home office anyway, so that an examining accountant can get a pretty good idea of what is going on.

Probably, as a rule of thumb, any picture showing net profits or about at the break-even point should be audited, just on general principles. Most of the time an auditing accountant will find enough discrepancies, which the distribution company will acknowledge, to justify whatever fee is charged. Perhaps some accountants will even take such a matter on a contingency fee arrangement.

Advertising

It is usually axiomatic that a distributor has complete charge of

109

advertising, publicizing, and promoting the film. Ordinarily distributors do not want to give the producer the right of approval or even consultation on advertising. Once in a while, a smaller distribution company may give the producer the right to develop an advertising campaign, subject to the distributor's approval, and will provide for this in the contract. Certain producers have their own concepts of advertising and certain expertise in their field, and when they make a deal with a distributor, they will condition the deal on having the picture advertised and presented the way the producer envisages. Very few producers have such bargaining power, however.

The agreement will ordinarily give the distributor all ownership rights in the advertising and publicity material, including any rights to merchandise characters from the film. Merchandising involves the sale of articles relating to the picture to the public. The sale makes money and helps promote the films. Successful merchandising in connection with most films is very difficult and only a few films (such as Disney and James Bond) have generated much merchandising income. Many of the distribution companies do not have an active merchandising department, and ordinarily merchandising gets an insufficient amount of attention in the distribution of a photoplay. Some independent organizations specialize in merchandising, but shy away from motion picture merchandising because most pictures do not lend themselves to any kind of merchandising. Even when a picture does lend itself to merchandising, merchandisers are reluctant to make a deal with a motion picture distributor and to spend the substantial sums of money necessary to develop and market a product, unless it appears fairly certain that the motion picture is going to do enough business to attract people to the merchandised products. There are some independent producers who have a flair for merchandising and a distributor is wise to let such a producer negotiate agreements with merchandising concerns as freely as possible.

Ordinarily, a distributor will manufacture certain advertising accessories, such as lobby displays and billboards, to help promote the motion picture. The distributor tries in the P-D to elect that either income from the sale of accessories goes into gross receipts and the expenses of the accessories are distribution expenses, or that the distributor keeps all income and cannot recoup any

110

expense as distribution expenses. Most accessories, as well as trailers, are loss items, so a distributor would do better financially with the former election. However, there is usually only a small amount of income involved, and to simplify accounting statements many distributors prefer to retain the income and not charge the expenses as deductions. Distributors try to preserve their right of election in the contract because it may pay for a distributor to take alternative positions in different territories. In addition, a distributor that does not handle its own distribution overseas may find that its own subdistributors insist that advertising revenue be included in gross receipts and advertising expenses be deducted as a distribution expense; such a distributor will try to impose that election on its producers.

The mechanics of preparing an advertising campaign are quite simple. The advertising department will prepare a concept either by itself or in conjunction with an outside agency and will ordinarily contract the actual preparation of the artwork to one or more independent agencies. Sometimes more than one potential campaign is prepared, and, ultimately, a selection is made by the distributor. The one selected is then printed in various formats and the ads are reproduced in the form of a press kit which contains the advertisements and publicity material. The press kits are sent to exhibitors, who use them in advertising the picture, along with the biographical material, publicity material, tie-ins, and whatever else the distributor thinks is going to help promote the picture. Outside companies handle the manufacture of the advertising accessories, which are ordered directly by the theatre exhibitors. The press books contain various samples of advertising and the mats and the plates for these samples are kept by the company so that all the exhibitor has to do is to pick up the phone and order directly whatever he wants.

Assignment of Rights in P-D Agreement

In a P-D, consideration must be given to a clause limiting the producer's right to assign his proceeds. Most P-Ds will provide that the producer cannot assign the net receipts until delivery of the picture to the distributor. The distributor believes that if the producer can assign the net receipts prior to delivery, then the

111

producer may have no incentive to finish the film and make delivery. Ordinarily, agreements will give the producer the right to assign receipts after delivery of the picture, provided that 1. the assignee signs an agreement confirming the distributor's rights in the photoplay, 2. if the distributor has a claim against the assignor, the distributor will not have to pay the assignee, but can offset against this claim, and 3. the assignee has no independent right to audit. If there is more than one assignment, the distributor will ordinarily have the right to appoint a disbursing agent so that the distributor does not have to render accountings to several people.

Some distribution companies want a preferred right to acquire the producer's interest in net receipts of the photoplay if the producer wishes to dispose of them. The distributor with a hit film showing net receipts for the producer will argue that he should have the first refusal or the last refusal to purchase those receipts, since the distributor helped make the picture profitable. Whether or not a producer should agree to this clause may, among other things, involve a tax question. Net receipts can be sold as part of the stock or assets of the production company so as to achieve a capital gain. This potential tax-saving device may not work if only the net receipts are acquired by the distributor. In addition, it may be advisable that the receipts be sold to a tax loss corporation, and a particular distributing company may not be in this position.

Many of the concepts inherent in the negotiation of a production financing and distribution agreement are also involved in alternate forms of financing a motion picture. It may be that an independent producer cannot get a major motion picture company interested in his production, or may not want to be burdened with the restrictions imposed upon him by the major distributor. The independent producer would then search for other forms of financing, some of which will now be considered.

Chapter Six

OTHER FORMS OF FINANCING

Other popular forms of financing a motion picture production include a *limited partnership agreement, a negative pickup agreement including territorial sales and advances for rights, and government financing.*

A. LIMITED PARTNERSHIP

The limited partnership agreement is presently the favorite form of organization for the procurement of private financing, whether raised from friends or through a public offering.

The standard theatrical limited partnership agreement provides that the investors—that is, the limited partners—receive 50% of the net profits and the producer, or general partner, receives the other 50%. It is customary that the investors recoup their investment prior to the general partner sharing in the profits.

Motion picture limited partnership agreements are slightly different than the standard theatrical limited partnership agreements in that there are various ways of providing when the profits will be shared by the general partner and the limited partners. A few possibilities to consider are the following:

1. In the event the film goes over the budget and additional financing is secured, does the person who furnishes the additional financing receive priority in repayment before the original limited partners?
2. Will the limited partners be repaid their capital contribution in full prior to payment of deferments and others who participate in gross or net receipts?
3. Are payments for talent from the net profits payable off the top, from the limited partnership share of profits, or solely from the general partner's share of such profits?

Of course, in the limited partnership agreement, the parties may agree to any resolution of these questions, but this must be set forth clearly in the partnership agreement. Whether or not the talent will receive a preference, or the limited partners, or persons responsible for the completion money will depend upon the respective bargaining power of the parties.

One ought to bear in mind that it is not unusual for the limited partnership agreement to also provide for a producer's fee and reimbursement to the producer of any other expenses that he will incur in connection with the production of the film.

With the trend to low-budget film-making in the not-too-distant past, someone was bound to come up with the idea of financing films in a manner similar to the way Broadway shows are financed. This has become an increasingly popular method of financing low-budget films, and when a film is done by an independent producer without the assistance of a major studio it might be considered the most common method at this time.

The producer of the film becomes the general partner of a limited partnership in which the producer shares one-half of the net profits (usually it is half, although it may vary) after the total investment of the limited partners has been repaid to them. Since the producing entity is usually a limited partnership, the liability of the investors is limited and the investors enjoy the tax benefits of being partners. Unlike stockholders in a coporation, the profits are only taxed once and not taxed as income to the corporation and again as dividends to the stockholders. In the event of a loss, the loss may be considered a capital loss. Most investors in films have more need of a loss which can be offset against ordinary income than they have for a capital loss.

As of September 1, 1963, it became possible for a New York corporation to be a general partner or a limited partner. This means that it is possible to combine the advantages of a corporation and the advantages of a partnership by having the producer or producers first organize a corporation which becomes the general partner of the limited partnership. In this way, the investors, being limited partners, would have all of the tax benefits of a partnership and the producer, at the same time, would enjoy the advantage of limited liability, since the producer, as a stockholder, would not be exposed to general liability.

If the corporation has large assets and is substantial, there may be good reason for doing this. If, however, a corporation becomes a general partner of a limited partnership and the corporation has no assets to speak of (and the Internal Revenue Service has rules to determine the assets which the corporation is required to have), then the Internal Revenue Service would consider the partnership to be in fact treated as a corporation for tax purposes. In this event the investors would lose their ordinary income deductions and the other tax benefit in the event of a profit. The producer should consult his attorney to determine whether or not it is likely that the Internal Revenue Service will consider the entity a partnership for tax purposes.

Even if the corporation as general partner has no assets, there is nothing to prevent an affluent producer from convincing one of his less affluent co-producers to be the general partner of a limited partnership together with a corporation belonging to the affluent member. As long as an individual is one of the general partners, there is no tax problem with a no-asset corporate general partner.

One ought to also bear in mind that in order for a partnership to be taxed as a partnership and not as a corporation, it must, in fact, have certain basic characteristics. And there are four characteristics of a corporation that distinguish it from other entities: 1. continuity of life, 2. centralization of management, 3. free transfer of the interests, and 4. limited liability.

115

It is not easy to set forth fixed rules to determine whether the entity will be considered a partnership or corporation for tax purposes. Each of the characteristics of a corporation has relative importance and in making a determination all of the factors are taken into consideration. If all four characteristics of a corporation are present, there is no doubt but that it would be a corporation for tax purposes; however, if less than all four are present, it may or may not be considered a corporation depending upon a number of factors which are impossible to detail here. Suffice it to say that one must be aware of the problem so that the partnership does not end up inadvertently being treated as a corporation for tax purposes.

As stated, it is most usual that the limited partners—that is, the investors—receive 50% of the net profits of the partnership. There are instances in which the producer may have difficulty financing the movie and may find it necessary to give the investors 60% of the net profits.

It is also most usual to provide that the partnership will not be formed and the funds invested will not be used until the amount necessary to produce the film has been raised.

If the limited partnership is actually formed in New York State, it is necessary to file a *certificate of limited partnership* with the County Clerk in the county where the business has its office. It is also necessary to publish the certificate or the substance of the certificate once a week for six successive weeks in two newspapers in the county in which the original certificate is filed. The County Clerk will designate the newspapers and one is always the *New York Law Journal*. The budget for the film should include the cost of legal advertising, which can range between $200 for one or two partners, to $1,000 for 50 to 60 partners.

Other states may have similar statutory provisions which must be complied with to effectively organize limited partnership.

SEC Registration

If the producer wishes to have a public offering in interstate commerce, it is necessary to file with the Securities and Exchange Commission. A public offering is not always easy to define; however, it does mean an offering to persons who are not close friends of the offerer and who may not be sophisticated investors.

Raising money in interstate commerce means simply that the producer will seek to obtain monies from persons outside the state where the business is to be organized. The basic problem with the offering is its expense, both in legal and printing costs, in relation to the amount of money wished to be raised. If the registration is unsuccessful the costs incurred must still be paid.

If it is determined that the producer will need to obtain money in a state outside the state where the principal business is and will be seeking to obtain funds from the public, then the producer must either have a full filing with the Securities and Exchange Commission or may make an application for exemption from registration, which is known as a *Regulation "A" exemption.* The determining factor is the amount of money that will be raised. If less than $500,000 is being raised, the exemption from registration may be obtained; if more than $500,000 is to be raised, the full registration is required.

One should not be misled into thinking that an exemption from registration does not require filing some documents. All it means is that the documents that must be filed are less voluminous and somewhat less complicated than the documents that must be filed for a full registration, and should be accepted for filing faster.

An exemption from registration may be filed with a local Securities and Exchange Commission office; that is, if one is operating in New York City the application may be made to the local office in New York City. The full registration must be filed with the Securities and Exchange Commission office in Washington, D.C.

An exemption from registration requires filing of a document entitled a *Notification Under Regulation "A,"* and certain exhibits. The exhibits will consist of an *offering circular* and a copy of the limited partnership agreement, as well as any other contracts which may have been entered into in connection with the film at the time of the filing.

The offering circular must be given to every person the producer wants to approach for the purpose of raising money. For this reason the offering circular will contain a good deal of information that one might consider to be discouraging to investors. It is the intention of the Securities and Exchange Commission to make sure, if at all possible, that there be a full and fair disclosure of all of the pertinent facts surrounding the offering. The Securities and Exchange Commission is probably less interested in what the terms are, or what any arrangement may be with prospective investors, than in insuring that prospective investors have full information to assist them in determining whether or not they wish to invest in the film.

The notification under Regulation "A," like all of the other documents, is submitted to the Securities and Exchange Commission in quadruplicate.

This document must set forth the name of the producer, the name of the producing company that will be organized to produce the film, the date the company will be organized, the state in which it will be organized, and the state in which the principal business will be carried on.

The offerer must set forth any predecessors, affiliates, and principal security holders of the issuer, as well as their addresses and the nature of the affiliation. The name of any person owning 10% or more in the producing company must be set forth as well as the amount of such interest.

The name and residence of each director, officer, and promoter of the offering company also must be set forth. One should bear in mind that many of these requirements are particularly applicable to a corporation, and are inapplicable to a limited partnership, which would be the producing company in many such low-budget film ventures. For example, a limited partnership which would be the issuer would have no officers or directors.

The names and addresses of the counsel for the issuer and the counsel for the securities underwriter, if there is an underwriter, must be set forth. For a limited partnership offering an underwriter is usually not used, so this would also be inapplicable. The issuer must state if he, his predecessor, or any affiliate issuer has been convicted of any crime or offense involving the purchase or sale of securities; is subject to any order, judgment, or decree of any court temporarily or permanently restraining or enjoining such persons from engaging in, or continuing any conduct or practice in connection with, the purchase or sale of securities; or is subject to a U.S. Postal Service fraud order.

The notification must list information concerning the promoter,

118

general partner, or principal security holder of the issuer, and must state whether or not any of them have been convicted of any crime or offense involving the purchase or sale of any security, or arising out of any such person's conduct as an underwriter, broker, dealer, or investment advisor; are subject to any order, judgment, or decree of any court enjoining or restraining such persons from engaging in or continuing any conduct or practice in connection with the purchase or sale of any security, or arising out of such person's conduct as an investment advisor, underwriter, broker, or dealer; have been or are suspended or expelled from membership in any national or professional security dealers' association or national security exchange or Canadian securities exchange; or are subject to a U.S. Postal Service fraud order.

There must be set forth in what states or provinces the offering will be made, and, if it is to be made by advertisements, mail, telephone, or otherwise, the method which will be employed in those particular states or provinces.

There must be set forth information as to any unregistered securities issued by the issuer or any of its predecessors or affiliated issuers within one year prior to the filing of the notification.

Whether or not the issuer or any affiliated issuer is presently offering or contemplates offering any other securities in the U.S. or Canada must also be described in detail.

The notification will set forth a list of the other exhibits which are being submitted together with the notification, such as the offering circular and limited partnership agreement.

SEC Full Registration Pursuant to Form S-1

The *registration statement* consists of a *facing sheet* of the form, the *prospectus* containing certain specified information, certain other information required which is largely inapplicable to a film financing, and the exhibits.

The Facing Sheet

The facing sheet sets forth the name of the issuer; that is, the name of the limited partnership and the general partner or general partners, since it is the limited partnership, through the general partners, which is offering the securities (limited partnership interests). In addition, the nature and amount of securities being

119

offered is indicated. Thus, for example, if the partnership is capitalized at $750,000, $750,000 in limited partnership interests would be stated. If the general partner is entitled to 50% of the net profits of the company, and the limited partners the other 50%, then the price per unit is, for convenience, figured on the basis of 50 units. In a partnership capitalized at $750,000, each unit would cost $15,000 and would represent a 1% interest in the partnership. (Bear in mind that the producer receives 50% of the net profits for no investment.) The filing fee and the name and address of counsel to the issuers are indicated and a statement is added that the approximate date of the proposed sale is as soon as possible after the effective date of the prospecuts (the date of clearance with the SEC).

The Prospectus

The prospectus (also referred to as an offering circular), being the basic sales document used in connection with the sale of securities to the public, must contain all of the relevant facts concerning the offering. As with the offering circular under a Regulation "A" exemption, no sale can be made unless, prior to the sale, a prospectus is shown to the potential investor. The prospectus must be prepared with great care and accuracy since misstatements, even though unintentional, may be serious and cause the issuer to incur liability.

Although no sales may be made until after the prospectus has been accepted for filing with the SEC, while the SEC is processing the offering, a *red herring* prospectus may be distributed to potential investors. After the prospectus is initially filed with the SEC, a legend in bold red ink is printed across the top of the first page as follows:

PRELIMINARY PROSPECTUS—ISSUED

A registration statement relating to these securities has been filed with the Securities and Exchange Commission, but has not yet become effective. Information contained herein is subject to completion or amendment. These securities may not be sold nor may offers to buy be accepted prior to the time the registration statement becomes effective. This prospectus shall not constitute an offer to sell or the solicitation of an offer to buy, nor shall there be any sales of these securities in any state in which such offer, solicitation or sale would be unlawful prior to registration or qualification under the securities laws of any such state.

This red herring prospectus (which may be used with a full registration but not with an exemption from registration) may be sent to potential investors to advise them that an offering is being processed and that sale will be made in the future. It is important that a detailed record be kept of when and to whom the red herring is distributed, as such information will be requested by the SEC.

Contents of the Prospectus

The prospectus will contain all of the facts of the partnership agreement, information about the persons involved in the production, and facts that SEC regulations require to make investors better informed.

Other SEC Information Required

There is a large mass of information which must be accumulated and furnished to the SEC for their purposes, but does not appear in the prospectus. Much of this information is intended to inform the SEC about the conditions surrounding offerings other than film offerings and is particularly applicable to corporate offerers. For this reason, many of the items are inapplicable to a film production, so the information is furnished by stating that the items are inapplicable. The exact information required is carefully prepared by the attorney for the production, and a detailed itemization is beyond the scope of this book.

"Blue Sky Laws"

In addition to filing with the SEC, most states require that an offerer file certain documents with a state agency. In the event that the offer is solely within a state and not in several states, then the filing may be required in that state.

Since securities laws (known as the *Blue Sky Laws*) of the states vary considerably, it is beyond the scope of this book to describe each of the filings. In all events, one should be aware of the fact that it might be necessary to file in several states and that under certain curcumstances, an exemption from the filing may be acquired in certain of those states.

B. NEGATIVE PICKUP

One form of financing a movie production is by means of a negative pickup agreement, in which certain territories or rights (such as television or non-theatrical) are licensed to a distributor in return for an advance, usually payable partly on execution of the agreement, but mostly on the delivery of the film. The concept of a negative pickup deal is very simple, even if the agreement does get very complicated. A distributor for a particular territory or territories or for particular rights will agree to pay a producer a stated sum of money upon delivery of the completed film. Usually the sum is an advance against a percentage of the gross or net receipts of the film. The reason for the deal is quite simple. The distributor gets a completed picture containing certain agreed upon elements for a fixed sum of money (usually less than the production cost) or no money at all. The distributor runs no risk that the picture will go over budget, for if it does, the responsibility for over-budget costs is the producer's. In addition, since the distributor pays only a small portion of the advance upon the execution of the agreement, the distributor risks relatively little if the film is not delivered. The producer, on the other hand, has a contract which obligates the distributor to pay him a stated sum of money on delivery of the film, or at least to distribute it, and this may be important to potential financiers of the film who will know that at least there are distributors for the film.

The producer will want to use the contract (if an advance is to be paid) as collateral for a bank loan that will provide the financing required to make the picture. When the film is completed, the bank is repaid from the distributor's payments. The usual problem involved in negotiations for a negative pickup deal stems from the fact that the producer wants an agreement with the distributor which is self-executing. In other words, if the distributor delivers

A, B, C, and D, then the distributor must pay the producer X dollars and distribute in accordance with the agreement. The distributor will always want to have a few loopholes in the contract so that if the picture is really awful, he may reject it. Of course, if the contract gives the distributor the loopholes, the contract is not bankable, since the bank cannot be sure of payment, even if the film is delivered, and it cannot be used to finance the film.

It is essential in a negative pickup deal that the agreement describe exactly what it is that the producer must deliver. Ordinarily, the producer will agree to deliver a motion picture based upon a script which the distributor has approved and which will be directed by a named director with certain designated people as stars. In some instances, the distributor will also want to approve of the budget so that he will know that the producer is going to spend at least a certain amount to produce the photoplay.

Sounds simple—but do not jump to that conclusion. In the first place, there is usually a deviation from the shooting script in the completed picture. Things will happen on the set from day to day that require a certain amount of rewriting. A certain scene just may not look right when photographed as written. In a negative pickup deal, the producer must always worry that if he is making too many deviations from the script, the distributor may reject the finished picture for not being in conformity with the script.

Another problem can occur if the agreement provides that certain named persons will direct and star in the film. If one of the persons dies, the distributor may be able to get out of the contract. The producer can obtain cast insurance covering the death and disability of the director or a principal member of the cast, and if the director or a principal member of the cast is disabled, the producer might ordinarily get a replacement. But if the distributor does not approve of the replacement, the producer must either wait until the disabled person is better, or risk forfeiting the negative pickup deal. From the point of view of the cast insurance company, it may be more economical to replace a disabled director or cast member than it would be to wait until the disabled person is cured. Thus, there may be this conflict between the producer's cast insurance requirements and the negative pickup agreement requirements unless the cast insurance specifically

123

covers the loss incurred by the producer in losing the negative pickup deal.

There is also a problem in obtaining financing for any over-budget costs, that is, the costs in excess of the pickup price. If the negative pickup agreement is going to be the collateral for a bank loan or a loan from a private investor, then the bank or investor must be assured that there will be sufficient money to finish the picture over and above the investor's or the bank's loan, for if the needed money is not available and the picture is not finished, there will be no pick up. The deficiency may be cured if there is a completion bond, but ordinarily the bond, as has been seen, is difficult to obtain and an independent producer may have to provide an assured source of additional financing if it is necessary.

From the independent producer's point of view, if a negative pickup agreement sets forth terms of a certain artistic quality for, the film, the concept could be so intangible and subjective that the distributor could refuse to pick up the film on the grounds that the picture was not of the quality standard named. Therefore, the producer should insist that the agreement should set forth standards in terms of technical quality, because a dispute of technical quality can be resolved by a competent laboratory. For instance, the agreement could provide that the distributor will put a stated sum of money in escrow in a bank, or issue a letter of credit drawn on a bank, payable on receipt by the bank of a letter from a laboratory to the effect that it has certain stated film material and that the material is of a quality sufficient to strike commercially acceptable release prints. The letter of credit could contain other requirements, such as a notice that the shooting script was identical to, or substantially identical with, the originally approved script, together with a certification that the approved talent had actually appeared in the film in their roles and that the approved director had actually directed the film. This is the ideal arrangement for the producer, but will not be greeted with enthusiasm by most distributors.

So, although simple in concept, the negative pickup deal is usually difficult to work out. If the deal is going to be banked by the producer, very often either the producer or the financier is extremely naive and willing to take less than perfect papers. If the producer has the risk capital required to make the photoplay, and the agreement does not have to be banked, then the producer may be better off waiting until the film is finished and trying to make a better deal with a distributor later.

If the distributor pays a fixed sum for a film, how are over-budget monies recouped? Assume that the distributor has agreed to pay $700,000 on delivery of the photoplay and the producer has managed to spend $750,000. Does the producer recoup the $50,000 he spent in excess of the budget in proportion to the $700,000 advanced by the distributor, or is he in second position, after the distributor has recouped? Since the distributor had agreed to pay for a picture costing $700,000, the distributor may take the position that the producer should recoup his money only from the producer's net receipts from the film. These questions must be resolved in the bargaining.

C. OTHER METHODS OF FINANCING

Another method of financing is government or territorial financing. Occasionally, a government will agree to furnish certain production costs in return for distribution rights in a given territory. For instance, the Soviet Union sometimes will agree to furnish a certain stated amount to make a film in return for the distribution rights within the Soviet Union. Of course, under these circumstances, the government putting up the money will usually want the production made within its borders. Ordinarily, a large part of the costs supplied by the government will be in the nature of barter, since it will consist of below-the-line costs, such as the furnishing of certain stipulated personnel, machinery, equipment, or the right to photograph at certain locations. Similarly a talent may waive part of a fee in return for the rights to distribute the completed film in a particular territory in which the talent is popular.

This type of financing is somewhat different from the British EADY plan, described previously. With the EADY plan the producer must find the financiers, but then receives a payment based on the amount of theatrical gross receipts within the territory of the United Kingdom. In this form of government financing the government pays the producer a certain stipulated sum of money that goes directly into the production. Even though the producer may lose the territory, there is no great loss if the territory is one that is not normally sold.

It is sometimes possible to finance part of the cost of a production through a laboratory that agrees to do the head-end work—that is, the manufacture of dailies and other preprint materials—for a discount, or for a deferment of part of its costs. Similar agreements may be worked out with respect to the use of production equipment. To the extent that any of the major motion picture distributors have studios that they wish to keep utilized, it might conceivably be possible to secure studio facilities on an arrangement that the studio will recoup some of its costs as a deferment. If a laboratory or a studio utilizes its overhead, and the producer pays less than the going rate, this is in the nature of a discount. As an alternative, the laboratory or the studio might provide a proportion of the financing in return for the producer's agreement to use the studio facilities or the laboratory, or perhaps any financing required in addition to the advances obtained from territorial sales.

Obviously, no one type of financing is used exclusively and there are also many combinations of the various types of financing arrangements.

Chapter Seven

PRODUCTION AGREEMENTS WITH TALENT

Once an independent producer has the money to finance the film, the cast and budget have been selected and approved, and it is time to start principal photography, there are certain production contracts he will use in the making of the motion picture.

One of the most important agreements is the talent agreement. Within the U.S., all experienced film actors are members of the Screen Actors' Guild, and an independent producer must become a member of the Screen Actors' Guild and execute the Guild's Minimum Basic Agreement. The minimum basic agreement describes in great detail the salaries, rights, duties, and obligations of actors, depending upon the amount of money they earn and the minimum time period for which they are hired. Certain actors hired on a day-to-day basis or a week-to-week basis are hired by means of a form approved by the Screen Actors' Guild (SAG), and the only deviations permitted in that form are certain matters not covered by the guild agreement, such as billing credits. Most attorneys do not get involved in the preparation of the Screen Actors' Guild approved contracts for those actors, and the casting

127

director or production assistant will ordinarily prepare them and have them executed as a matter of routine. An attorney will prepare certain riders to the agreements for use in the event that an actor is to receive billing on the screen or in paid advertisements and in the event the actor has bargained for items in excess of the guild minimums. The SAG form agreement relates to the minimum basic agreement, and the minimum basic agreement should be referred to for working conditions, overtime, and other conditions of employment.

In dealing with lead actors who are paid more than the guild minimum, most of the major motion picture distributors use a long form of artist agreement, since the guild does not have an applicable standard form contract for that purpose.

The elements of an actor's agreement are quite simple. Ordinarily, an actor is hired for a certain consecutive minimum period of time, starting on a certain date, and will receive a stated salary, usually a stated sum per week for the minimum period, whether or not he is actually required for all of the minimum period. If the actor has not completed his services within the minimum period, the producer will have the right to extend the minimum period for an indefinite period of time, paying a sum for each additional week, or part of a week. Actors receiving large salaries are sometimes hired for the production schedule plus two to four weeks so that the possibility of over-weeks is reduced.

Sometimes, there is a free period between the expiration of the minimum period and any additional extended period, during which the actor will work without pay. The concept of the free period is for the actor's benefit. If an actor is required for 12 weeks and is to be paid $12,000, his agent may insist that the actor be hired for a minimum period of ten weeks plus two free weeks. Instead of being paid a thousand dollars a week for 12 weeks, the actor will receive $1,200 a week for ten weeks. The actor will benefit if there is an additional period of employment after the 12 weeks, because traditionally the additional weeks are paid for at the same weekly rate for which the actor was originally hired—that is, for $1,200 rather than $1,000 per week. The agent can also say to third parties that his client received $1,200 a week and not $1,000 a week, which is helpful for the actor in negotiating for the next film job.

128

Ordinarily, although this point may be negotiated, an actor will render services for the producer after completion of principal photography, subject to the artist's availability, to balance the sound in the event that the actor's voice does not come through properly, and rerecord some of the dialogue if necessary. The first to the third day of such services are usually without additional compensation. Usually, an actor will render services for a period of from two days to as much as two weeks prior to the start of the minimum period, also without additional compensation, for rehearsals, publicity, wardrobe fittings, and the like. Any time period more than one week is usually the subject of negotiation, both as to length of time and compensation. An important point to consider is the starting date of each actor. If the actor is a principal who is needed throughout principal photography, the starting date is presumably the first day of shooting. However, some actors are not needed for all of principal photography, and if their starting date is fixed too soon, they may end up sitting around and getting paid for doing nothing.

Sometimes an "on or about" date is used, with as big a swing period before and after the date as the producer can negotiate. Note that with actors hired by the day or from week to week, the starting date and any variation in the starting date are governed by the Screen Actors' Guild Minimum Basic Agreement.

The producer will ordinarily have the right to recall the actor for the shooting of additional scenes after completion of principal photography if necessary, in which event the actor will generally receive weekly payment proportionate to the weekly salary originally received. The recall is of course subject to the actor's availibility. The producer may also require that the actor be available for publicity photos, appearances, and the like, after completion of principal photography of the film. Usually the actor receives only transportation and living expenses for these services.

According to the terms of most talent contracts, the producer can require the actor to work indefinitely, as long as his services are required and the actor receives his weekly compensation. The fact that an actor may be required for more than the minimum period may require an actor to change the planning of his activities. Sometimes, the actor will try to forestall the changes by insisting that after a certain date he will no longer be required to render services for the producer, whether or not he has completed his services. This date is called a *stop date*. Sometimes the stop date is flexible in that a producer will receive an extension if a delay in filming which necessitates additional shooting is caused by an Act of God or the actor's disability. This stop date provision is potentially disastrous for a producer, if principal photography is running behind schedule. If the actor leaves, the producer will have to suspend production until the actor is available again. The alternative is to rearrange the shooting schedule to finish photographing the actor's scenes, and this always increases costs, since scenes are being shot other than planned. Consequently, most producers will strongly resist any imposition of a stop date and any conflict of engagements is usually resolved informally by the parties involved. Usually, an actor will try to schedule his engagements far enough apart so that he can be sure of completing one before he starts another.

An actor's compensation is almost always paid weekly, usually on the Wednesday or Thursday following the completion of the week. If the actor works for a period less than a week, his salary is prorated. The usual formula is six days for work at locations and five days for work in the studio. The number of hours an actor may be required to work and the rest period between the time the actor stops working and the time the actor is required to start the next day is regulated by the Screen Actors' Guild and is set forth in the guild agreement. To the extent possible under the guild agreement, the producer will try to provide that if the actor must work overtime, he will get additional time off at some later date, rather than receive additional compensation for the overtime.

Besides compensation for services, an actor ordinarily will receive reimbursement for living expenses if he is working at a place sufficiently removed from his residence to necessitate overnight accommodations. This can either be stated as a reimbursement to the actor of "first-class living expenses" or "ordinary and necessary living expenses," or it can be stated in terms of a fixed amount of money per week to reimburse the artist. The living expense allowance will vary, depending upon where the film is being photographed. For instance, if principal photography will take place in New York City and in an upstate community in New York State, the producer may argue that the actor should not

130

receive the same living allowance for the upstate location because it is much cheaper to live there. For the metropolitan area, the actor's living expenses might be one sum, and for rural areas it might be another.

In addition to the living expense allowance, the artist ordinarily will receive round-trip transportation from his residence to the place that principal photography is to occur and from one location to another. With principal artists, the agreement will almost always provide that the transportation will be first-class and by air if air transportation is available.

In addition to the basic living expense allowance, important artists can and do demand a host of other things. These can include round-trip transportation for more than one—perhaps the artist's spouse and family. It can also include specifications for private dressing rooms; a private trailer for dressing on locations; the artist's personal hairdresser, makeup man or double; a chauffered limousine to transport the artist to and from locations; etc. Sometimes more time is spent negotiating these fringes than the actor's remuneration. It is important to bear in mind that all of the fringe benefits payable to the artist, such as living expenses, transportation, and the like, can add up when figuring the cost of production of the film. In these days of low-budget films, it is surely more difficult for an actor to obtain the type of living expense allowance and accommodations that he would have received without question in better times.

We have been discussing the services, which the producer and actor will usually agree, the actor should render. There are some services which the artist may want to render, but which the producer may not want to use. For instance, the agreement will almost always provide that the producer has the right to dub or use a substitute actor to record the dialogue for foreign languages, and to dub the artist in English if he is not available or unable to perform. For instance, there may be songs in the role that the artist cannot sing. Some actors want the right to do the dubbing of their performances in certain other languages. If the artist is going to do this kind of dubbing, the producer will want to provide that it must be without compensation, because the actor's salary will in all probability be greatly in excess of the compensation that would be paid to anyone else doing the dubbing. Also, if the dubbing is going to be done in a foreign country, the producer will not want to be obligated to pay for transportation of the artist to and from the foreign country in order to do the dubbing. This could be very expensive; the total cost of dubbing an entire film rarely exceeds $30,000 for dubbing into English, $5,000 for dubbing into French, $3,000 for dubbing into Italian, $10,000 for dubbing into German, and $2,000 for dubbing into Spanish. Furthermore, the agreements between the distributor and subdistributor may permit the subdistributor to dub the film into the language of the territory, and it is possible that an agreement with the actor to do the dubbing might violate such agreements.

Some agreements will require that the artist receive substantial prior notice whenever any dubbing in English is going to take place so that he will have an opportunity to be available. Most actors will not want their role dubbed by an incompetent actor or someone whom the actor deems to be second-rate, and if any dubbing in English is necessary the artist may want some right to approve whoever is to be used. The producer will also want the right to use a double for the artist to perform hazardous acts and perhaps to appear in scenes in which the artist is not readily recognizable. This could cut down the artist's minimum period, and it also might save the artist from injury. Most artists will not object to this, but there are some artists who insist on performing their own stunts. In such a case, the cast insurance company must be notified immediately and an additional premium may be required, because most cast insurance is based on the fact that the principal artists will not be asked to do anything dangerous.

All form agreements will contain variations of two key clauses, which may be considered together. The first key clause will state that all of the rights to the results and proceeds of the artist's services belong to the producer, and the producer may do anything he wishes with those results and proceeds. The second key clause is the pay or play clause, which provides that as long as the producer pays the artist the compensation required under the agreement, the producer is under no obligation to play the artist, that is, use the artist in the film at all, or he may use only selected portions of the film in which the artist appears. Thus, it is possible for the artist to sign for a leading role and find that most of his performance has been left on the cutting room floor. If the artist is hired for a role and during the shooting is found to be unsuitable, the producer can in essence fire the artist merely by paying off his contract and substituting some other actor to fill the role.

To protect the importance of their role and to insure the artistic quality of the film, some important actors insist on and get certain rights of approval from the producer. A star may want to approve the final script, the director, and possibly the other principal actors, or at least the actor with whom he will be sharing the lead. Sometimes various formulas are utilized to secure the artist's approval. The producer picks a certain number of names and the artist selects one (or vice versa). The producer and the artist mutually agree on a list and the producer can hire anyone on the list. Such approvals create special problems for the producer even if the producer is willing to grant the approval in principle. For instance, if the artist has script approval and approves a final script, what happens if some rewriting is done during the course of the production, as is always the case, and the artist does not like the rewriting? Has the producer breached the agreement?

One compromise is to provide that the importance of the artist's role will not be significantly or substantially changed during the filming or cutting. Such a subjective test could, however, result in litigation if there is a disagreement between the artist and producer. If the artist approves the director or star, and the director or star must be replaced because of death, disability, or default, does the artist have the right to approve of the substitute director or star? Could the artist leave the production on the grounds that his approval of a substitute has not been obtained? To the extent such approvals of substitutes must be given, one solution is to make the artist agree that the approvals must be given if certain objective conditions are met, for instance, that the artist must approve any director who has directed at least two films, each of which has earned a certain amount as gross receipts, or had a budget of a minimum amount, or the substitute actor is of similar stature as the actor who must be replaced. Another solution for the producer is to restrict the actor to consultation privileges only, rather than approval, with the producer having the final say. These solutions take into account the fact that at the point in time when the producer or financier is investing large sums of money toward the production, the producer must know that the actor is committed. Of course, the actor will in fact have approval of the script, at least to the extent that the script is usually complete when the actor sees it, and if he doesn't approve he simply doesn't take the job. It should be understood that revisions can be made in the script during principal photography without the artist's approval. This is most customary in the business.

Most artists resent the pay or play clause and the fact that the producer has the right not to use a performance. To the extent that the artist can get the producer to agree that the script cannot be changed materially without the artist's approval or that the importance of the actor's role cannot be decreased as opposed to some other actor, then the artist will have some assurance that his performance will be preserved after principal photography has been completed. These rights of approval by a star are very, very rare, however, and ordinarily an actor must accept the fact that his performance can be cut and that he cannot contractually control the artistic quality of a film.

Among the rights granted are commercial tie-up and merchandising rights discussed in connection with the P-D agreement. However, the artist will insist that his name or likeness not be used in connection with an endorsement of a product or service.

The agreement will give the producer various reasons for not paying an actor, such as *force majeure*, or an Act of God. If production of the film is halted because of a *force majeure*, such as a fire, strike, flood, riot, insurrection, war, or other occurrence beyond the control of the producer, including the death or disability of the director or star, most talent agreements generally provide that the actor's performance under the agreement is suspended for the period of the *force majeure*. An actor should make sure the items set forth in the agreement are in fact similar to those stated and that *force majeure* is not defined as an act beyond the control of the producer.

Ordinarily, during the period of suspension, the artist may work for a third party. As a practical matter, it is very difficult for an artist to arrange other employment on such short notice, and, in all events, the producer will want the artist to be subject to recall on short notice when the *force majeure* has ended. To protect the

134

artist, the agreements commonly provide that if a suspension lasts for a stated number of weeks, either the producer or the artist has the right to terminate the agreement, except that the artist cannot terminate if the producer starts paying the artist compensation under the agreement. The number of weeks can be anywhere from four to eight, depending upon the bargaining position of the parties.

Ordinarily, the agreement will provide that if the artist cannot provide services for a stated period of time because of disability or incapacity, the agreement can be terminated by the producer. The shorter the period of time, the better it is for the producer. The period of time usually is anywhere from three to ten consecutive days to ten to twenty-one days in the aggregate during principal photography. The agreement usually provides that during such illness, the artist would not be entitled to receive compensation, or render services for others, but if he remained on location during the illness, he would be entitled to living expenses. If there is a dispute between the producer and the artist as to whether or not the artist is ill, the producer by contract usually retains the right to have the artist examined by the producer's doctor, and the artist's doctor may attend the examination. Ordinarily, the cast insurance company's doctor will also want to examine the artist.

If the artist breaches the agreement, the producer usually will have the right to suspend the artist for the period of the breach and a reasonable period of time thereafter to reassemble the elements of the film. If the artist takes several days off and does not show up at all on the set, and for that reason the producer has suspended the production of the film, then the mere fact that the artist later shows up ready to perform should not obligate the producer to put the artist back on salary unless the producer is actually ready to proceed with the production. Sometimes this period from the date the artist reports to the date the producer is ready to proceed with the production is expressed in terms of a number of weeks in which the artist can remain suspended, such as four or six weeks. During any such actor-caused period of suspension, the producer will insist upon the right to terminate the agreement, obtain injunctive relief in the event the artist wants to work elsewhere, recover damages caused the producer by the

135

artist's breach, withhold compensation, and eliminate the artist's billing credit.

What constitutes a breach by the actor is not always easily ascertainable. It is necessary to distinguish between a material breach of the agreement and a non-material breach. A non-material breach, for example, might be the artist's reporting 15 minutes late for a day's shooting. Even though the producer ought to have all of his remedies at law, such a breach is not really a material breach and should not be grounds for termination of the agreement. Sometimes an actor's agent will try to provide that the actor has a 24-hour period to cure any breach. Some breaches can be cured, but some really cannot. If the artist shows up drunk on the set, or does not show up at all, there is a breach that cannot be cured. With a 24-hour grace period, the artist could fail to show up every other day and still not be in breach of the agreement. In reality, about the only way the artist can breach the agreement is by not rendering services at all, or by violating a clause, such as the morals clause, which will be discussed later.

It is more difficult to establish that the artist is breaching an agreement because he forgets his lines or has to have each scene reshot an inordinately large number of times. For this reason, no matter what the agreement provides, the producer is generally at the artist's mercy. If the artist attempts to win a dispute with the producer by fluffing lines, the artist will get what he wants depending on how badly he is needed by the producer.

The talent agreement will generally provide that the producer has the right to obtain injunctive relief against the artist in the event of the artist's breach, but how long should that right continue? If the artist wants to render services for third parties after the mimimum period, should the producer still have the right to prevent his working? The producer's position is that as long as the artist is not rendering services for the producer, the artist should not render services for anyone else.

The actual damages the producer will try to include can be astronomically high if a production must be suspended while an artist is in breach of the agreement. A producer will definitely not want to pay the artist any compensation in the event of a breach of the agreement. The big problem arises when the producer and artist disagree as to whether or not the artist is in breach. The artist will rarely admit that he is in breach. The producer will want to provide contractually that if there is a disagreement, the producer can withhold money, deposit it in court or in a special bank account in trust, pending the outcome of the dispute. The artist will not want the producer to have that right. If the producer does not pay the artist, and has no right to withhold or deposit, the producer will run the risk of being in breach himself if it is later determined that the artist never was in breach in the first place. If the producer cannot withhold or deposit, he has a dilemma. If he refuses to pay the artist and a court decides he was wrong and should have paid, he is in breach himself. If he does pay and a court rules that he was right and need not have paid, he may never be able to get the money back. It is very difficult to collect money from an individual who is not working steadily, and the artist can frustrate legal attachments by putting money in someone else's name, by setting up a corporation, or by assignments which may prevent the producer from collecting a judgment. On the other hand, if the producer is operating as a dummy corporation and the corporation may not be able to pay a claim, then the actor may insist that the contracts be guaranteed either by the financier or by the distributor. This is another of the many disputes in which the settlement depends upon the party's bargaining power.

What happens in the event the artist is entitled not only to fixed compensation, but contingent compensation such as either a deferment or a profit participation, and the artist's services are terminated after he has completed a small part of his role? Does the artist receive in addition to the prorated portion of the minimum compensation due prior to the termination, a prorated part of the contingent compensation, if the photoplay is completed and released? In other words, do part of the contingent payments become vested if there is a termination for reasons other than a breach prior to the completion of services, or must all services be completed before the contingent compensation rests?

Some agreements provide that if the artist appears in his role on the screen, he must be paid in full including all contingent compensation. To the extent that the artist's services are covered by cast insurance, if the artist is disabled, cast insurance would pay the producer not only the minimum compensation to the artist, but any other contingent compensation provided to be paid by the producer to the artist. This would mean that in the event the artist were contractually entitled to receive a deferment or a participation and the artist was disabled but the producer used footage of the artist in the film, the cast insurance would cover those payments to the extent they represented part of the producer's loss under the policy.

From the producer's point of view, if the termination is caused by an Act of God, not covered by insurance, the producer will have lost money and there is some reason for him to take the position that the artist should also lose. Ordinarily, if there is a *force majeure* suspension, production of the photoplay is generally never completed, so that the whole question of paying contingent compensation based on the release of the picture is academic. This is not necessarily so if there is a cast incapacity, particularly if the incapacity takes place at the beginning of a production. It is most often possible to substitute for an actor or director and continue with the production of the film. As noted, the decision whether or not to continue with production or terminate, although made by the producer, to a large extent is influenced by the cast insurance company.

Because of the importance of cast insurance, most agreements will provide that the artist must be able to be insured by cast insurance, and that the cast insurance can be obtained from the insurer without special conditions and with no more than the normal deductible for policies of that type (usually $10,000 per event of disability). Note that almost anyone can be covered for cast insurance, but the insurance policy will exclude known illnesses or other personal defects. For example, if the actor has a history of back trouble, the cast insurance policy will exclude any disabilities resulting from a bad back. In such a case the cast insurance coverage would be excluding the one thing the producer would want most to be protected against. All contracts should contain a provision that the actor will truthfully complete any insurance forms required and cooperate with the producer so the insurance can be obtained.

Although the cast insurance policy may not have any special exclusions, the deductible may be increased to an unreasonably high figure, or the premium may be higher because of an additional risk. If the actor has had claims on previous pictures, this would also affect the rate. The agreement should provide that the cast insurance must be obtained before the artist starts rendering services, and if for any reason usual cast insurance cannot be obtained and the producer wants to terminate (and he should have that right), the termination should take place within a short time after the producer is notified about the insurance, or the producer should forfeit his right to terminate the agreement. Also, if the cast insurance policy can be acquired only if an additional premium is paid, then the artist should have the right to pay the additional amount of the premium to keep the agreement in effect. In the event there is an increased deductible, the artist might want the right to pay the producer the difference between the regular deductible and the increased deductible if there is an injury.

The cast insurance policy will usually provide that the artist, during rendition of his service, cannot engage in any extra-hazardous activity or fly on any non-scheduled airline without the written consent of the cast insurance company. If the artist should be called upon to engage in such hazardous activities, a special policy is usually written. Special policies can also be obtained that cover transportation on airlines, whether scheduled or non-scheduled.

Every agreement for services should contain, from the producer's and distributor's viewpoint, a provision that in the event the producer breaches the agreement, the artist's rights and remedies are restricted to an action at law for damages, and in no event will the artist have the right to enjoin distribution of the film or its advertising and promotion or to terminate or rescind the rights granted. The reason for this clause has been discussed in connection with P-Ds.

There are various ways that actors will try to modify this clause. The artist may try to get the producer to agree that if the producer or distributor breaches the agreement concerning the artist's advertising billing, the artist will have the right to enjoin the offending ad, for it is usually impossible for the artist to prove damages under such circumstances. How can the artist possibly prove that billing 50% of the size of the title of a film instead of 75% of the size of the title has caused the artist monetary damages? It is, of course, possible for the agreement to provide for an amount of liquidated damages in the event the billing clause is violated, but such a provision might well be regarded as a penalty clause, which under the law would be unenforceable.

In addition, as previously said, it is common for exhibitors to completely ignore the approved advertising billing. Further, if the advertising billing of the artist is violated, the costs involved in manufacturing new plates of the ad and reprinting the press book are quite substantial. Also, newspaper and magazine space may have been purchased and if new ads have to be prepared, there may be nothing to run in the newspapers. The situation is much worse if the error in billing occurs on the main title of the photoplay.

The agreement also provides that no termination of the agreement can deprive the producer of the results and proceeds of the artist's services. In other words, if the producer terminates because of an Act of God or breach by the artist, the producer always wants to own that portion of the artist's services that was completed before the breach. The performance may still be salvageable.

Most agreements will provide that the artist must furnish modern wardrobe items to the extent that the artist has them in his possession, and also that the artist must return to the producer any costumes furnished to him. Ordinarily, however, the producer will furnish all clothing and it is not unusual for the producer to let the artist keep the clothing furnished if it has not been rented.

Most producers and distributors will insist that an artist not issue press or publicity releases about the film without the prior approval of the producer or distributor. The reason for this is simple. If the distributor has a national advertising and publicity campaign which the artist may be totally unaware of, a casual statement by the artist to a particular reporter might rob the whole campaign of its impact. Since the artist is ordinarily not aware of or party to the producer's and distributor's publicity plans for the film, neither the producer nor the distributor will want the artist interfering with the campaign.

Most talent agreements contain a *morals* clause, in which the producer is granted the right to terminate the agreement in the event an actor commits any act which is contrary to public morality or tends to shock or offend the community or ridicule public morals. The clause is inserted to protect the producer against adverse publicity which might affect the box office success of a film. However, the clause is generally written in a broad manner and covers not only criminal acts, but even political acts and other conduct which might not even constitute a crime. The clause has not been utilized on many occasions, and the general bargaining technique is to make the clause as specific and narrow as possible. To the extent that the clause is worded in terms of acts that might "tend to" subject the actor to public disrepute or ridicule, the "tend to" language should be eliminated. Instead of the producer being granted a right of termination, he is sometimes limited to the right to remove the actor's name from screen and advertising credit, but is still obligated to pay the actor.

There are some actors who object strenuously to the whole concept of such a clause, and will insist on having it removed completely. These actors regard the clause as a personal insult. Whether or not a producer will agree to remove the clause entirely depends upon the actor's general reputation and whether or not the producer actually feels that this actor's misconduct can harm the potential box office of the film.

The question of billing credits in an artist's contract is usually very complicated, and of great importance to the artist. There are two types of billing credits: 1. on the screen on all positive prints, and 2. in advertising. Billing credits on the screen means that the name will appear on the negative and all positive prints of the film.

It would be helpful to define some of the terms used in the industry in connection with billing credits. The *main titles* of the film are the titles that ordinarily appear at the beginning, together with the title of the film, and the *end titles* of the film, as one might guess, are the titles that appear at the end of the film. In the past, all of the credits customarily were on the main titles of the photoplay, and the only credits appearing on the end titles were a list of the cast credits indicating the roles played by each principal member of the cast and possibly a studio credit.

Today, the credits tend to be interspersed with the action at the beginning of the picture, and there is also a tendency where permitted by guild agreements to have more credits at the end of the picture. It seems that more and more people are becoming entitled to credit whether by guild agreement or by custom, and the credits seem to be getting longer and longer each year.

One must consider whether or not the credit is going to be based on a percentage of the size of the title. The title is ordinarily going to be the largest single lettering in the advertising and in the main title, and the artist will want to be billed in relation to the title if possible. An alternative would be for the artist to be billed in proportion to the size of the credit to another artist, to a director, or to a producer. This would mean that the title can be any size and could result in a gigantic title and very small credits to all of the individual artists. The distributor will want to sell the picture with as much freedom as possible, and will not want to have to give prominent credit to people whose names will not sell tickets to see the picture. Some factors to consider are the following:

1. Is the percentage of the credit based upon the size of another credit or the size of the title?
2. What is the position of the artist's credit?
3. Is the credit above or below the title of the film?
4. How many artists can be billed ahead of the artist? If the artist is going to be in third position, may the artist in first or second position be above the title of the photoplay, and not the artist in third position?

One must also consider not only size but color, boldness, prominence, style of type (the type face used may contractually have to be the same as the title), and spacing between credits. Color and style of type are fairly objective, but prominence and boldness are certainly subject to interpretation. In addition, the credit can be given prominence by appearing after the word "and", or "as (name of role)," or by appearing with a box around it.

Will there be a provision (most rare) obligating the distributor to use the artist's likeness in connection with advertising of the photoplay? This is called a *likeness* clause. Here the problems are enormous. Are the sizes of the likenesses to be the same? What relative position does each get? More commonly (but still rare), there will be a provision that if anyone else's likeness is used in an

142

ad, the likeness of the star must also be included. The artist's agent always fears that after a hard bargaining session for proper billing for his client, the ads will appear featuring some young girl whose picture undoubtedly draws people to the box office, but detracts from the billing of the artist. Obviously, actors suffer from this more than actresses.

Recently, the use of an "art-form" title has been gaining acceptance in the industry. This kind of a title is a stylized title, followed by a regular title. The artist's billing will not be based on a percentage of the stylized title, but on a percentage of the use of the title under the stylized title. This will enable a distributor to have a very large stylized title, and to have the artist's billing based upon a smaller, non-stylized use of the title.

Ordinarily, any obligation to the artist for billing credit will contain exclusions for certain types of advertising, such as advertisements smaller than a certain number of column inches in newspapers and magazines. Ordinarily, the exclusion is for eight column inches, but it can be six, and rarely four. Group or list advertising, in which a number of pictures are listed together in an ad, is usually an exclusion also, as is a teaser ad. A teaser ad is a "coming attractions" ad. Ordinarily, billing in trailers is also excluded.

Other advertising exclusions relate to Academy Award advertising in which a particular artist receives an Academy Award nomination and the advertisement is geared just to that artist, or an institutional advertisement relating to the distribution company, or advertising in narrative form. Advertisements in radio and television are excluded from billing requirements and so is the mention of the artist's name in publicity releases. If the artist has sufficient bargaining power, he sometimes insists that the artist be billed even in excluded ads, or if any other person connected with the photoplay is mentioned in any of the excluded advertising or publicity, the artist's name must also be mentioned. Some of the agreements provide that a casual or inadvertent failure to comply with the provisions of the advertising agreement will not be a breach of the agreement.

Sometimes for tax purposes the artist, like the producer, will not want to be an employee but will have his own corporation, which will lend the production company the services of the artist.

The loan-out agreement would then be for the corporation to cause the artist to perform the various services for the producer. The loan-out agreement will ordinarily contain a provision warranting that the artist has entered into an agreement with the corporation pursuant to which the corporation has the right to lend the artist's services. In addition, since the corporation will sign directly with the production company, the artist will be required to sign a loan-out ratification in which, among other things, he makes the same warranties, representations, and agreements as the corporation, and agrees that if the corporation does not do what it is supposed to do and "cause him to perform," then he will work directly for the production company.

As a practical matter, from the producer's view the two types of agreements are the same, and the only reason for entering into the loan-out agreement would be to accommodate the artist. From the artist's point of view, under the loan-out agreement, the lending company is responsible for the payment of any guild pension and welfare payments, as well as for the payment of social security and the like. Ordinarily, the artist will insist that the production company pay the equivalent of any such guild pension and welfare payment and the like to reimburse his lending company for these payments.

The artist or the lending company will also try (but will rarely succeed) in obtaining a tax indemnification clause in the agreement in the event that the film is going to be produced outside of the U.S. Such a clause would provide that the artist be reimbursed to the extent that his income taxes are greater because he must render services outside the U.S. The production company must always be extremely careful to determine in advance exactly what the artist's income tax position is and what the extra tax liability might be.

Chapter Eight

DIRECTOR'S AGREEMENT

In many respects, a director's agreement and an actor's agreement are similar. The clauses with respect to billing (with the exception to be mentioned later), breaches, *force majeure*, illness, and such are pretty much the same. The principal differences will relate to the starting date and the scope of the services of the director. It is quite rare these days for a director to be hired for a specific starting date and for a specific number of weeks.

The reasons for this are numerous. With directors having more and more artistic control, the director will be vitally interested in the preproduction work on the film and will surely have very definite ideas about casting and the script. By the same token, a producer will not want to make a commitment to a director on a pay or play agreement in which all of the director's compensation vests, until the producer is sure that the film will definitely be made. Consequently, many director's agreements are arranged in two stages, a preproduction stage and a production stage. The director will in the first stage agree to work for a stated compensation in the development of the screenplay and in the casting of the film. From the director's point of view, the problem with this arrangement is fixing a time during which the director will be sure that he is going to direct the film and by which the producer will become responsible for paying the director's fixed compensation, whether or not principal photography is commenced.

This may be resolved in a number of different ways. The agreement may provide that if the director has not been given a starting date by a certain specified time, he has the right to make other engagements. In this event either the producer must wait until the director has completed the other engagement before fixing the starting date, or the agreement will terminate, and the producer will have to hire another director. As a variation, the agreement may provide that the director can take other engagements after a certain specified date, except that before doing so he must first advise the producer, who would have the right to preempt the engagement. In this case the director would receive a starting date and his compensation would become vested. The agreement might provide that if the starting date were not fixed by a specified date, the agreement would automatically terminate and the director would keep whatever compensation he had been paid. This type of arrangement would achieve the greatest flexibility for the producer. He would have the advantage of having the director do the preproduction work (script, budget, cast, etc.) for what is usually a limited sum of money, therefore minimizing his risks. Of course, if the director left the project and another director was hired, that director might want to do different preproduction work and might have different ideas about the script.

After a director begins working on a film, he may find that there are problems with the script that he did not anticipate, or that his concept of what the completed photoplay should be does not coincide with his producer's, and they may both want to be relieved of their obligations. The producer should ever be mindful of the fact that one of the most difficult parts of producing a film is arranging the various creative elements so that they will all be available at the same time.

After the preproduction stage has passed, and the director has been given a firm starting date, the other parts of the director's agreement are effective. Ordinarily, the director must work exclu-

146

sively on a film starting somewhere between four and eight weeks before the commencement of principal photography, leaving time to finish casting and generally to get the production into shape.

Although some agreements may provide that the director is entitled to payment for working additional weeks of principal photography after a certain stated number of weeks, most agreements will now provide for a flat fee and that a director's services are exclusive throughout principal photography. The reason for this is simple. Ordinarily, if there are problems with the principal photography of the photoplay, it is the director's fault. If the director is slow in shooting or requires many retakes and principal photography is delayed, it would seem unfair to permit the director to benefit from his own inefficiency by paying him overweeks.

Payment of compensation to the director is usually handled in a manner somewhat different than with the artist. The director will receive a stated amount of money during the preproduction period and will not be entitled to anything else unless he is given a firm starting date. At the time he is given a start date, the rest of his compensation will ordinarily become vested. Usually, this compensation is payable in equal weekly installments during the approved shooting schedule, but sometimes a percentage of the compensation will be held back until the director has completed cutting. Quite frequently, the director will be entitled to receive either a deferment, a profit participation, or both.

Because there is usually no provision in a director's contract for overweek payments, the *force majeure* suspension requirement, to the effect that after a certain time either compensation must be paid or the agreement is terminated, would not be applicable. The reason is simple enough. If we assume that there is a *force majeure* suspension of 12 weeks, and the agreement provides that after eight weeks either the actor or the producer can terminate unless the producer begins paying the actor, if the producer does not want to terminate, he would have to pay the actor for the four weeks when he was not working. Since the actor is hired for a minimum number of weeks, then, under these circumstances, he would receive four additional weeks, or four overweeks of payment. But not so with a director if the director is prepaid a flat sum for principal photography no matter how long it takes.

Ordinarily, the length of time a director can be ill during

147

shooting without causing a termination of the agreement is somewhat more generous than the illness provision for an actor since the director will render services for a much longer period of time.

Under the Directors' Guild of America Minimum Basic Agreement, after completion of principal photography the director has the right to one cut of the photoplay. Many scenes are shot many different times from varying angles, and, ordinarily, not in sequence. After everything has been photographed, the scenes must be cut and assembled to make the most effective motion picture. This is also called *editing*. Although there are film editors who specialize in cutting and editing photoplays, more and more directors are coming to the realization that no matter how well the actors are directed and the film is photographed, the director can lose control of the completed product if he does not retain the right to supervise the editor and cut and edit the film. Though the guild requires the director to have at least one cut, it is not unusual for a director to request two or three cuts.

It is most important for the producer to make certain that the cut is completed within a rather short period of time. With the high cost of money, the longer it takes to release the film, the more interest will run, and the more difficult it will be for the film to make money.

Ordinarily, it will take anywhere from six to twelve weeks to complete the first cut, depending on how fast the director works and how complicated the shooting was. Some directors will cut while they are shooting. Sometimes there is a public preview between the cuts, so that both the producer and the director have the opportunity to gauge the public's reaction and to determine whether the scenes in the film have the desired effect. All time periods ought to be carefully spelled out in the contract and it should be provided that if the director does not complete a cut in the required period, he will lose all further cutting rights.

In addition, the director ought to be contractually obligated to work exclusively during the time he is cutting the photoplay, or at least his services to the producer should take precedence over services to others. Since the director will want the right to cut the photoplay, there will usually be no provision that he be paid extra for the cutting, and the flat sum paid to him will cover all of his services.

148

In the event that the director has obtained artistic controls over the photoplay (and a director as well as a producer can have these controls), these would be spelled out in the provision of the agreement, which otherwise ordinarily would provide that the producer has the right to direct and control the director's services. The controls and the exercise of the controls would be similar to the type of controls a producer would have in the production financing and distribution agreement. Of course, if the director and producer both have controls and rights of approval, there must be a method of resolving disputes between them.

In the event that the director receives a possessory credit in billing, such as "John Smith's *Hamlet*," there may be a dispute between the Writer's Guild and the Directors' Guild as to the propriety of such a credit for the director, since the Writer's Guild feels that this credit would detract from the screenwriter. However, the guild has permitted "A Film by" or similar credit.

The salaries of a director will usually range from a minimum of between $35,000 and $50,000 to a maximum of $500,000, sometimes more. The Directors' Guild agreement is concerned mostly with the director's creative rights in cutting, his billing credits, pension and welfare plans, and residual payments. The Directors' Guild agreement is not concerned with the day-to-day work rules in the same way as the Screen Actors' Guild. For example, a director's agreement will almost never provide that the director must work a stated number of hours, or any particular number of days in a week. Most directors understand that it is necessary to work all the time. They must be ready to set up the first shots in the morning, and in the evening they usually look at the completed film as well as prepare for the next day's work. It is most usual for the director to work unusually long hours.

Chapter Nine

PRODUCER'S AGREEMENT

In the event that an individual producer does not have his own production company, or is employed by a production company, or is not responsible for packaging, then an individual producer's employment agreement form will be used instead of a P-D. The differences in the form from a director's or artist's agreement are relatively few.

There ought to be provision in case of abandonment, so that the producer who comes with the literary property will have the right to repurchase the property if the film does not proceed as provided in the agreement. The extent of the producer's rights of approval or rights of selection should be spelled out in the provisions of the agreement, as would be in the case with a director. Since most individual producer deals are step deals, the agreement must state when payments are to be made and when the total producer's fee would become vested. The agreement, like the director's agreement, should make provision for what happens if the production of the film does not begin within a stated period of time. Would the individual producer be free to take on other assignments, and how would a conflict of assignments be resolved?

151

An executive producer's agreement will usually be similar in form to an individual producer's agreement, except the former will maintain only a supervisory function and does not have the day-to-day responsibilities of the production of the photoplay. For this reason, the duties of an executive producer are almost always non-exclusive, so that he will have the right to engage in other duties while acting as executive producer of a film. In some cases, the executive producer will have no duties in connection with the film, and the billing of "executive producer" is more of an honorary credit.

Chapter Ten

THE STUDIO AGREEMENT

Most photoplays, whether or not produced in this country, are made at least in part in a studio. Even the photoplays that are made largely on location will generally have some interior shooting, and ordinarily this is done in a studio.

There are two types of studio agreements most generally used. The first is a *studio facilities agreement,* in which a major producer-distributor owning its own studio facilities will enter into an agreement with an independent producer for the use of those facilities. If the major producer-distributor is the financier of the photoplay, you may rest assured that under normal circumstances the P-D will provide that the film must be produced at the studio of the distributor. In such a case, either a specified percentage overhead charge is made for the use of the facilities, or a more detailed facilities agreement breaking down the specific charges is embodied in the P-D, or in separate agreements between the producer and the distributor.

The other type of studio agreement that may be entered into is for an independent studio. Such studios exist in most major cities where any substantial amount of television or motion picture

153

production occurs, and of course there are specific charges negotiated and detailed in the agreement for the use of the various facilities of the studio.

In the case of a studio facilities agreement, the producer's cost for the studio will, of course, depend on the parties' bargaining power. The producer will want to get his production financed, and when the distributor includes a studio facilities deal as part of the obligation to pay for the cost of production, the producer may not be able to do much about it. If the studio charge is going to be based on a percentage of the budget or of the cost of production, the producer must find out to what extent the percentage is realistic and representative of the cost of the services being provided by the studio. Of course, the producer should find out what services are going to be provided. To the extent that the financier-distributor would like to assess an unreal charge which does not in some measure represent services, the producer must assess the charge to decide whether the P-D deal is worthwhile to him, or whether so many artificial charges will only insure that the film can never be profitable as a practical matter.

With an independent studio, the producer can bargain differently with his source of money for the film and can shop around more freely to see whether one studio deal is as favorable as another. He can also compare the facilities of the various studios to see which is best suited for his particular needs. In other words, in dealing with the independent studio, the charges are always negotiable with the bargaining power of the parties being dependent upon the number of independent studios in the vicinity, and how busy they happen to be at the time. If the studios are loaded with work, the producer can bargain very little, and if the studios are empty, he will be in a better position to work out a desirable agreement.

Chapter Eleven

THE STUDIO FACILITIES AGREEMENT

The studio facilities agreement of a major motion picture financier-distributor will provide (barring the unusual) that all studio work must be done at its studio. The agreement will set forth exactly what facilities will be made available, and if the producer does not know precisely what he will need, a production manager must be consulted to make certain that the needed equipment will be available.

Ordinarily, the studio will permit a producer to use only its stage facilities, equipment, and material, unless the studio cannot provide what is required. In addition, the producer may be required to execute guild agreements and wherever possible to use the studio's employees. If the producer has any specific personnel he wishes to use on the film, he must make these facts known and so provide in the agreement.

Some contract provisions will apply to both a studio facilities agreement with a major studio and an agreement with an independent studio. One such common provision is the period of the lease. When will the studio facilities be required, and is there a

fixed termination date? Ordinarily, the studio will charge a different rate for construction purposes, for shooting purposes, and for
striking purposes (that is, removal of the sets after completion of
shooting). It should be borne in mind that rent will be paid for a
particular day, whether or not the studios are used, so the producer should plan carefully. In fixing a termination date, the
producer must be protected in case principal photography extends
longer than anticipated and the studio is needed for additional
periods of time. Under most circumstances, there will be provision
for an outside cutoff date so that the studio may know that on
some specified date the facilities may be rented to another producer.

In either agreement, it is important to consider exactly what
portions of the studio and what items of equipment are being
rented. Ordinarily, these items will be enumerated in a schedule,
but in addition to the particular sound stages and other major
shooting facilities the studio will be providing, there must be
arrangements for access to and use of offices, makeup rooms,
dressing rooms, carpenter shops, and possibly parking facilities. If
there is a particular time of day which the studio must be used, or
if the producer wants the studio available at all hours on a
seven-day-a-week basis, the agreement must so provide and must
require that electricity, heat, etc., are available during the needed
periods.

Most studio leases will contain a clause requiring the producer
to pay any sales tax payable on the rental covered by the agreement. There may be a question as to whether or not the sales tax
is payable on the entire cost of the rental, or whether part of the
cost should be apportioned between real property and personal
property. Some services provided by the studio may be exempt
from sales tax, so if the studio insists on inserting a clause
obligating the producer to pay the sales tax, then the producer
may be able to arrange to indemnify the studio for taxes actually
paid, or to pay whatever taxes are due directly to the government.
If the charges of the studio are deemed to be manufacturing costs,
then an exemption certificate from the local jurisdiction can be
obtained and in such event the studio will not charge a sales tax.

Usually, the studios will require the producer to obtain liability insurance, insurance against loss or damage to the equipment, fire insurance, and workmen's compensation. Normally, the producer will be obligated to repair or replace lost or broken equipment unless the breakdown was due to normal wear and tear or a defect in the equipment when the producer received it. The studios will also try to limit their liability to their negligence or gross negligence.

The producer must also be alert to provide that if other stages in the studio are being used by other producers, there should be some control over noise and interference. The producer must rely on the studio to supervise the shooting to make sure that one production is not going to prevent another production from working.

Chapter Twelve

OTHER TECHNICAL AGREEMENTS

Most technical personnel engaged for the picture will receive weekly checks, and will not be hired for any particular minimum period of time. There are various guild agreements governing the services of such technical personnel which the producer will sign. The agreements provide for compensation, overtime provisions, and the like, and will occasionally contain billing credit requirements. On rare occasions a technical person well known in the industry may insist on a special contract. He will negotiate for a fixed number of weeks as a minimum no matter how long his services are actually required, instead of settling for employment on a week to week basis.

The form of most employment agreements for technical personnel is substantially like the form of the actor's contract. Many of the terms and conditions will be the same, except that usually an employment agreement will be a much shorter agreement and will not go into the same detail as an artist's contract.

Essentially, the agreement should provide that the producer is granted the results and proceeds of the employee's services and that the producer has the sole right to direct, supervise, and control the services of the employee during this period. The agreement should also state a minimum term of time period with a provision that if the employee's services are needed for additional weeks, the compensation will continue at the same rate for the additional period of time. By and large, most of the contract terms will be governed by the appropriate guild agreement, which will be incorporated by reference into the employment agreement.

In addition to employer-employee agreements, there are occasionally special agreements required to arrange for the case of extraordinary lenses or photographic equipment, such as Panavision. These agreements are usually in the nature of a leasing agreement, with the lessor leasing specified equipment to the producer at a specified cost. The agreement will generally require billing credit and will detail the rights and obligations of the lessee, particularly providing for rights and obligations if the equipment becomes lost, damaged, or stolen. It is usually difficult to achieve any substantial change in the lessor's clauses in this type of agreement, and by and large, extended negotiation of this type of agreement is not usually required, so long as it is clear what the costs are, and as long as most of the producer's risks can be covered by insurance.

Chapter Thirteen

MUSIC

There are several types of music that can be used in connection with a motion picture. First of all, music may be written specifically for the motion picture by a composer selected by the producer. Secondly, music which has already been composed and recorded can be used in the motion picture if a synchronization license is granted by the music publisher. The latter case is common, for instance, in trying to establish a time period; for example, if a picture is set in the 1930s, music from the 1930s would help create a mood to establish that period. Thirdly, there are some music publishers who will provide a producer with "canned" music, or music which has already been recorded, and which the producer can insert into the picture as required.

Music Originally Written for a Motion Picture

Ordinarily, the composer of music for a motion picture is not hired until after principal photography has been completed, at the point at which the director must cut the film. The music will serve to highlight specific scenes or episodes, and, though a composer could begin to write prior to any cutting, it is customary for him to wait until there is at least a rough cut so that he will have some idea what the motion picture is about, what type of music is required, and where in the film it is required. When the rough cut is completed, the composer can begin working out the main themes and considering the areas in which the music will be inserted, but the music cannot be matched to the picture until there is a *fine cut.*

There is usually a four to six week period from the completion of the fine cut until the music is actually recorded. There may be a number of recording sessions, so that the music is tailor-made to fit right into the appropriate segment of the picture.

Although the agreements will vary, the composer is usually responsible for arranging, orchestrating, and conducting at the recording sessions. In addition, of course, the composer will at the inception meet with the director to determine the concept of the musical score, where the music is going, and how it should sound.

There is no fixed minimum or maximum for a composer to write a score for a film, but the minimum is usually not less than $7,500, and the maximum can range to $25,000 and upwards. The agreement will generally provide that the composer is an employee of the production company; the production company will own the score and the copyrights in the composition as employer. To the extent that a score is published by a music publishing company (usually the publishing company of the financier-distributor if there is a P-D, or a publishing company selected by the producer or a distributor, depending on the deal), the composer will get the usual writer's royalties, as would any songwriter writing for a publisher. Some established composers have sufficient bargaining power to insist that they co-publish their scores with the music publisher of the producer and receive one half the publisher's share as well. These provisions are solely a matter of bargaining, and there is no always-applicable rule of thumb.

The music score is intended to enhance the picture, but in addition, the producer and the distributor are always hopeful that there will be one or more hit tunes in the score so that the publishing rights they obtain will become valuable. Under the actual agreement as an employee of the producer, the composer will agree to render exclusive services for a stated period and as

162

long thereafter as the producer deems necessary for the writing of the musical score. Sometimes the composer's compensation is based on a minimum number of weeks and he is compensated for overweeks. Sometimes, as mentioned, the composer will work for a flat sum, no matter how long it takes him to compose the score.

The composer will agree to confer with the producer and director when and where the producer may require. It is sometimes most difficult to fix a start date for the services of the composer because it will depend upon when the fine cut of the photoplay will be completed, and this is not always easy to know. Sometimes the agreement will provide that the composer's services are non-exclusive during the period from the rough cut to the fine cut, and in this period of time, the composer may be able to write the themes and other major parts of the score, although the actual scoring, as stated, will begin after the fine cut.

The amount of time the composer takes to compose the score directly affects the post-production schedule of the film. The faster the composer completes the score, the sooner recording sessions begin, and the sooner the film will be completed. In setting up the post-production schedule, it is always a good idea for the producer to provide that if the composer is late, or if his material is not satisfactory and other material is required, there is time to obtain it from another source.

The composer's agreement will usually provide that if the composer's material is not satisfactory, the composer will compose different material until the producer is satisfied. The composer will ordinarily put a limit on the number of times he must rewrite the score.

It is not uncommon for a producer to underestimate the amount of money required for music in the photoplay. If an original score is going to be written, a number of recording sessions will be requred. Many scores are recorded overseas, where costs of recording are much cheaper. Ordinarily, one or more sessions are held with a large number of musicians for that portion of the score requiring a full orchestra, and the balance of the sessions are held with a smaller group. In addition to the compensation the composer receives for composing the score, he will be paid the union scale for conducting, arranging, or copying, if he renders those services and union scale if he actually performs.

163

Sometimes union scale payments are applied against the composer's overall fee.

Many of the provisions which are usually found in the talent agreements discussed will also be in the composer's agreement. The composer's agreement will ordinarily permit the producer to have lyrics written for any music written by the composer, or to use new and different music in lieu of, or in addition to, that written by the composer.

If the score is published, the writer's royalties are payable to the composer, under the rules and regulations of the Composers and Lyricists' Guild of America Minimum Basic Agreement. These royalties are by and large the standard songwriter royalties of 6 cents per printed edition of a song, 10% of the wholesale price of the folios (prorated by a fraction, the numerator of which is the composer's song and the denominator of which are all songs in the folio, or all songs excluding public domain works), and 50% of record and synchronization income. In the event that there are lyrics written for any of the compositions, the composer's royalties are reduced to one-half, the other half going to the lyricist. The producer will try to insert a clause in the agreement to the effect that if the score is assigned to a music publisher, the latter becomes responsible for payment of the writer's royalties, and the producer's responsibility will cease. The agreement will also provide that there is nothing obligating the producer to have the score published.

In addition to writer's royalties, some composers who conduct will also receive the equivalent of a recording artist's royalty for a sound-track album, or singles derived from the sound-track album conducted by the composer. Whether or not the composer will receive such a royalty will depend upon the composer's bargaining power, whether or not he actually conducted, and whether or not he is a name in the recording field that will help to sell records. This royalty will range anywhere from 1% to 5% of 90% of the retail selling price of all records, manufactured, sold, and not returned, less excise taxes, cover and container charges. The 90% is to take into account a 10% figure for breakage. The 90% figure is still used, but there is no practical basis for it, since there is

164

ordinarily no breakage anymore, and broken records are accepted for return and not considered anyway.

If there is definitely going to be a sound-track album recording, it is probably a good idea to require the composer, when he scores the music for the film, to also do a separate score for the sound-track album. The effects required for the photoplay may not work for the sound-track album, the sound-track album (which will probably be sold to a different market) will most likely require a more modern, updated form of scoring, and most important, a sound-track album ordinarily requires fewer musicians.

Under the American Federation of Musicians' (AF of M) Minimum Basic Agreement, if music is recorded for use in one medium and is then used in another medium, all of the musicians involved in the first recording session will receive a substantial reuse payment. If there are 30 or 40 musicians at a session for the motion picture, to pay them an additional fee would usually be much more expensive than rerecording the music for a sound-track album with five or six musicians. Sometimes the two sessions are done at the same time, and sometimes the sessions for the sound-track album are done by the recording company when the album deal is consummated.

It is also generally much cheaper to record music outside of the U.S. because of the high cost of musicians here and the obligation to pay residuals in accordance with the union requirements. For various production reasons, however, this may be impossible, and in all events, the producer must always be conscious of the cost of recording sessions, studio charges, etc., in addition to the cost of the composer.

If the composer receives recording artist royalties, and the producer is not affiliated with a record company and licenses the album to a record company for a royalty, the producer will ordinarily agree that the composer and producer get paid on the same basis from the record company that makes the sound-track album. The producer must be careful to make sure that any royalty to the composer can be reduced if there are any royalties payable to other recording artists who also may perform in the

165

photoplay. In other words, if the composer is paid a royalty, together with a large number of other recording artists who are paid royalties, then the royalties payable can amount to such a sum that there is no longer any profit to the producer in making a sound-track album deal. The royalty is usually prorated and the fractional proportion paid to the artist featured on each band. If there are 12 bands, each band would be worth one-twelfth. If the conductor records all twelve bands and a recording artist performs on one of the bands, then the royalty to the recording artist is one twenty-fourth of the total royalty.

If the producer has his own record company, ordinarily the royalty payments of the record company will become part of the hiring agreement. Of course, that portion of the agreement is subject to negotiation in the same way that any recording artist's agreement would be negotiated.

The negotiating position for sound-track albums may differ from the usual record negotiation. A producer may be more concerned in the distribution of the record than in cash remuneration since the album is a selling tool. So a producer may exchange a cash advance for guaranteed presses of a minimum number of records, a minimum promotion sum, a record club deal, etc., and the release of the album would coincide with the release of the film for maximum impact.

As far as billing credit is concerned, the composer will receive billing depending on what he does. Making provision for billing in the agreement is not always easy. For instance, if the credit on the main title says "Music by" and there are musical compositions used in the picture written by other composers, then the credit is misleading. If the credit says "Music scored and conducted by," that credit may be accurate, but probably unsatisfactory to the composer who, if he wrote the music, also wants that fact known. The solution ordinarily is to have one credit for the composer and another card on the main title of the screen with credits for any composer or lyricist for songs not written specifically for the photoplay, and for any recording artist or recording groups. Sometimes the music cards will take up two or three separate cards on the main title of the photoplay. In addition, some composers command credit in paid advertising. Usually, the record company

166

releasing the record wants advertising billing also, since the ads help sell the records.

Once the score is written, or simultaneously with the writing of the score for the film, the producer may want another composer to write the title song. It is not unusual to hire one composer to do the underscoring and the background music, and a second composer to do the theme song of the photoplay. If the theme song composer or composers (if there is a separate lyricist) are well known and have written a number of hit songs, he (or they) can command a substantial fee ranging up to $5,000 or more, and possibly a percentage of the publishing rights for the song.

If there is a co-publishing agreement with any performer or composer in connection with the music, or any portion of it used in the film, then in addition to the usual provisions of a co-publishing agreement, the producer should obtain the right to use the music free of obligation to pay synchronization publishing royalties in connection not only with the film, but also for other photoplays or media in which the producer has an interest. Since the producer is paying to have the music written, it may be argued that he should not have to pay again if he wants to use the music in another context; however, this is a negotiable point and is not always obtainable.

Sometimes, a producer will feel that a well-known recording group or a recording artist singing the title song will add more appeal to the film and will help sell a sound-track album or singles. Dealing with the act can create substantial problems. First, whether or not the act has written the song, the act will probably insist upon a percentage of the publishing rights. Secondly, the act will certainly demand, in addition to a fee which can range from $5,000 and upwards, a recording artist's royalty which is usually 5% of the retail selling price prorated, subject to the various deductions as noted, or the royalty they receive under their recording deal with their own record company. The act will also insist on billing credits, both on the screen and sometimes in advertising, but this should be no problem, for the purpose of having the act in the picture is to publicize the picture.

Most acts are under exclusive recording contracts with a record company. That exclusive agreement may or may not contain a

167

provision that allows the act to record for another medium, such as motion pictures and participate in a sound-track album of the music from that picture. Whether or not the contract contains such a provision, the motion picture producer will in any event want the group to be available not only for the sound-track album, but also for a single record derived from the sound-track album. Unless the act has contracted for the right to do film albums with their record company, the group will ordinarily require a waiver from their record company, and such a waiver is generally very difficult to obtain. At best, the record·company will agree that it will permit the act to record the sound-track album, but may want to release the album on its own label. Surely it will want to release any single record of the act on its own label. This may make it difficult to deal with another record company.

In addition, assuming the act's record company agrees to release a single, the record company will want to approve the recording and the song to make sure the release does not harm the act. From the act's point of view, it will be paid a substantial fee to record music for the film. The act's record company does not share in this income. If the film is a success, the act will enhance its reputation. For the act, revenue from the sound-track album is incidental. On the other hand, if the song which the act records for the film is not a good song, the act's record company will not want it released at all and will certainly not promote it.

Ordinarily, during the negotiations the act's record company will say that it wants to hear the song and recording before making a decision on whether or not to release it. The agent for the act may tell the motion picture producer that the act controls what the record company releases, but this ordinarily is not entirely so. The record company in most cases has at least the right to approve what it releases.

The difficulty with permitting the record company to hear the song as recorded by the act prior to making a decision is that once the song is recorded by the act, the act is entitled to its compensation, and, furthermore, it is often too late to get another act to record the song. Also, if one act has recorded the song and the act's own record company hesitates to release it, other acts usually hear about it and do not want to record the song.

Even if the record company does agree to release a single

record, it is difficult, if not impossible, to obligate the record company to release the record as an "A" side. (Most single records have one hit side, the "A" side.) Usually record companies do not want to release a single record with a strong song on each side, on the theory that both songs will receive air play and that this division of air play will end up hurting the record sales, since the sides will compete with each other and may prevent the record from moving up on the record charts. Of course, two "A" sides on two records will sell two records instead of one. Usually, only the strong side (or the "A" side) is played and promoted by the record company. If the record company releases the song as a "B" side or throwaway side of a record, the song will not get air play and will not serve the purpose of free advertising for the film.

On the other hand, the record company will be interested in having the film advertise the record (as opposed to the songs advertising the film), and for this reason would rather wait until the film comes out to release the record. If the photoplay is a hit, the record company will promote the record; if it is not, the record company will do nothing.

The producer will, of course, want the record company to release the record sometime in advance of the release of the film so that the promotional effect of the record will have its maximum impact. It usually takes a record at the very least several weeks to get started.

Another complication is the fact that the record company will want to release its records of the act in a pattern. Ordinarily, if the act has a successful record in release, the company will want to wait until that record starts slipping off the charts before the follow-up records are released. This may directly interfere with the plans of the distributor to have the record containing the title song released prior to the release of the film. There is further difficulty in scheduling because the producer cannot tell very much in advance when the photoplay will be released. This is in the province of the distributor and may depend on such unpredictables as whether or not a particular theatre is available for the initial booking of the film.

For these reasons, it is usually very difficult to coordinate release of a single record of a hit-record act with the release of the photoplay for promotional purposes. If a number of pop acts are going to be used in connection with the photoplay, then of course it becomes imperative to clear all of the acts for a sound-track album.

The Sound-track Album Agreement

In today's market, it is unusual for a sound-track album of a film to have a large sale unless the film does substantial business. Generally, sound-track albums will not sell independently of the photoplay. Since the chances of great commercial success of any film is quite small, most record companies do not want to be bothered with the expense of pressing and promoting a sound-track album, unless they are sure that the sound-track is from an important picture that will do business.

The situation differs, of course, when the motion picture is a musical, and the sound-track album can have the same importance as an original cast album from a Broadway musical. There is absolutely no rule of thumb for the deal that can be negotiated for such a motion picture sound-track album.

With other kinds of albums, the royalty paid by the record company is usually somewhere between 7½% and 10% of 90% of the retail selling price, which includes payments to the recording artists. The record company will pay as an advance the costs of rerecording the album, or if there is no rerecording, any reuse fees payable, and this advance is recoupable from the producer's royalty payment. Sometimes an additional cash advance is paid. The producer is generally less interested in sales of the sound-track album than he is in seeing to it that as many albums as possible are disseminated. The producer will treat each album disseminated as point-of-sale advertising, and to the extent that the record company can guarantee store window displays, ads in consumer publications, or other forms of promotion, it will help the photoplay. The sound-track album should be and usually is released a few weeks ahead of the film for this point-of-sale advertising to have maximum effect.

It is for this reason that most producers (and for the purposes of the discussion the record deal can be made by the producer if he has retained rights, or the distributor if he has not) are less concerned about the provisions in record company contracts for reduced royalties or for "free" or "bonus" records than a record-

170

ing artist would be. The producer is interested in knowing that a minimum number of records will be pressed, that the records will be released in major foreign markets, that the record cover will contain a credit for the producer and the picture, and that the reverse side of the album cover will contain a synopsis of the plot, photographs, art work, and ordinarily credits for all personnel whose names will appear in paid advertising.

The producer will generally supply the art work to the record company and if he does not, he will want to approve the art work. He will also want to approve the description of the film appearing in the liner notes of the album. Ordinarily, the publisher of the music can negotiate to receive 24 cents per record as a mechanical license fee for the licensing of the rights to the music for use in the sound-track album. If, however, the album does not contain 12 bands of music, and many albums today contain only 10 or 11 bands, the record company may be able to bargain for a 20 cents or 22 cents rate per record (2 cents per band of music).

Since the sound-track album is so bound up with the film, there is ordinarily no difficulty in getting the record company to release the record album in conjunction with the release of the motion picture (assuming the company is interested in the first place), since there usually is no scheduling problem. But there may be difficulty in getting a release of the album outside of the U.S., depending upon whether the record company has its own subsidiaries or sublicenses abroad.

Prerecorded Music

Rather than having music written specifically for the film, because of the content of the film, it is sometimes decided to use music that was recorded earlier and not composed specifically for the film. This is true, for example, when a particular time period is being established, such as using an old standard hit song to establish a period feeling. Special problems may be involved in clearance of music for use with a film.

The music publisher of the music must grant the producer a *synchronization license*, which is a license to synchronize the music with the visual portion of the film, plus a theatrical performing license for the U. S., since the performing rights societies

171

in the U.S. do not license the use of the performance of music in movie theatres.

One should first find out whether the music to be used is copyrighted, in which case the license will have to be obtained, or is in the public domain. This will require either a search of the U.S. Copyright Office records, or an inquiry from the publisher or from the Harry Fox organization—a licensing agent of many publishers that grants synchronization licenses on behalf of its publisher members. If the copyrighted work is in the original term of copyright, there is an unresolved question as to what happens if the work enters its copyright renewal period and the publisher of the first term of copyright does not control the renewal rights in the U.S. It seems fairly well established that the synchronization license is a license which is granted in perpetuity, and the grant is complete when the music is fixed (or synchronized) with the photoplay. At least this is one theory, and the question has never been litigated, although there have been claims by publishers owning renewal rights from time to time. In any event, there may be a danger in acquiring synchronization rights to a composition near the end of the original term of the copyright. Of course, the question does not arise if the copyright is already in the renewal term, since the worst that can happen is that the composition enters the public domain, and this would affect the rights granted to the producer.

It is worth remembering that some compositions that are in the public domain in the U.S. are still protected in Europe, where by and large the copyright extends for the life of the composer plus 50 years. In addition to the 50-year term, various countries have enacted extension statutes, which serve to extend the copyright in compositions during periods of certain wars.

Even compositions written by Russian composers may be protected by an international copyright convention if there were simultaneous publication in Russia and in a country which is a party to the Berne Convention. Although it may be very hard to establish the copyright status of some music, it usually is not worth a lawsuit to prove that the compositions are in fact in the public domain.

The amount of the synchronization license fees for a composition will depend upon the business policy of the publisher and, of

172

course, the importance of the particular song. There does not seem to be any rule of thumb, but ordinarily a synchronization license will cost somewhere in the vicinity of $500 to $5,000 depending on the popularity of the song and the length and type of use. The producer will argue that the publisher may greatly benefit from performing rights monies earned when the picture is shown on television (and this is true mainly with network telecasts since performing income derived from the exhibition of a motion picture on individual television stations is usually not substantial), and exhibitions in movie houses overseas, as previously noted.

The license will specify the name of the musical composition, the name of the motion picture, the use made of the musical composition, the number of uses, and the length and type of use. For instance, if someone is singing the composition in the motion picture, it is a visual vocal use; if someone is playing the composition in the motion picture on screen, it would be a visual instrumental use, and if the composition is heard in the background, and no one is seen performing, it would be a background use, either instrumental or vocal, as the case may be.

The performing rights grant for television is conditioned on the clearance by the television stations of licenses from ASCAP or BMI. This generally is not a problem since every television station will have a license from ASCAP or BMI. However, if the composition is controlled by SESAC (Society of European Stage Artists and Composers), a third and much smaller performing rights society, there may be a problem since there are some television stations that do not license through SESAC. The radio stations throughout the country carry licenses from BMI and ASCAP, and most of them are also licensed by SESAC.

No mention is usually made in the license of "non-theatrical" uses. Most of the places (college campuses, auditoriums) where the photoplay could be exhibited non-theatrically will also obtain a license from BMI or ASCAP, allowing them to perform music there.

Some licenses will contain a restriction of the exhibition of the film for pay television. Of course, the producer must have the right to exhibit the photoplay for pay television, but some publishers are not willing to grant this right, on the assumption that they are entitled to a separate fee for such use.

173

Similarly, the status of rights for distribution of the photoplay in the form of cartridges is still undetermined.

Under the copyright law, a charge may be made for the use of music if the music is performed for profit. There is a question as to whether or not a performance of the picture by cartridge is a performance for profit. In any event, the producer cannot be in the position of having music in the picture with any restriction that may affect distribution of the film. Sometimes, the producer will insert a provision to the effect that if the photoplay is going to be distributed by new uses and if a fee is charged by publishers generally for such uses, then the producer may obtain clearance for such use upon payment of a fee equal to the fee generally charged by other music publishers. At least this formula will permit the use and set some kind of standard of payments for the producer.

Outside of the U.S., the synchronization license will generally provide that performing rights are cleared by the local performing rights societies, and ordinarily this does not create any problem. The license will usually provide that no change can be made in the lyrics or fundamental character of the music of the musical composition, that the title of the musical composition cannot be used as the title of the motion picture, and that the story of the musical composition cannot be used as part of the story of the motion picture. Payment for those uses would be more analogous to the acquisition of motion picture rights to a literary property. It may be necessary in distributing the motion picture overseas to translate the lyrics and substantially change the music. If there is going to be a translation, then at the very least the music publisher will want to own all rights to the translation. In some cases, the music publisher will want to write the translation himself, but if the use of the music is a visual-vocal use, then the translation, if there is going to be dubbing instead of subtitling, must be written to mesh with the lip movements of the singing. Fortunately, most music in photoplays distributed outside of the U.S. is sung as is, without dubbing. In other words, if someone is singing a song in English on camera, in the dubbed version the song will usually also be sung in English. If this is not the case, the synchronization license must be modified.

Unfortunately, the producer does not generally know in advance what will happen and whether or not dubbing will be required. Presumably, the publisher will agree to permit dubbing on condition that all rights to the translation are assigned to him and on further condition that the writer of the translation be deemed an employee of the producer or the producer's licensee, and would not be entitled to any songwriter royalties.

Most synchronization licenses will limit the music publisher's liability to the amount of the license. This limitation of liability is woefully inadequate if the music publisher warrants that he owns the rights and in fact does not. Generally, this particular point is non-negotiable.

In addition to the use of prerecorded music, it may be advisable to use an existing recording of music rather than hold an independent recording session to record the music. As stated, if there is a period flavor in the photoplay, the director may want to use an old hit recording to establish a mood. In some cases, the director may also want to use a symphonic composition which may already be recorded. Clearing rights of this kind may be most difficult.

In addition to the synchronization license, rights must be cleared from the record company that made the recording and the recording artists who performed the composition. There is no rule of thumb as to how much these rights will cost, but one problem is created by the fact that if the recording was made in the U.S., there may be reuse fee payments required to the AF of M. Whether or not reuse payments would be required and how much they would be would depend upon the agreement between the record company and the AF of M, which will depend upon when the recording was initially made. Most record companies do not bother to dig up this information, and if a reuse fee is payable, it is very difficult to determine how many musicians performed in the original record session and in fact who they were. If the music was originally recorded outside the U.S., this problem may not exist. But if the work is a symphonic work, the record company involved will probably want a good deal of money for the grant of permission to use it.

If the producer does not have money to go through the mechanics of creating an original musical score, there are companies that will provide background music for a film for relatively little or nothing. The company will provide the background music, the synchronization license, and the theatrical performing license for the music, but will retain all rights to music publishing and recording of the score. Ordinarily, the company furnishing the music will have the music composed very inexpensively or may have stock music which will suffice, and will have all music recorded out of the country, so that no rerun payments or residual payments are necessary. This will save the producer a good deal of money, but of course, the producer will generally not get as good a musical score, and will not have the benefit of whatever income can be derived from recording rights and from publishing the music, which, of course, is where the company furnishing the music hopes to cash in.

Chapter Fourteen

ACQUISITION OF DISTRIBUTION RIGHTS FOR COMPLETED PHOTOPLAY

A producer, rather than producing a film himself, or a distributor, rather than financing production to acquire distribution rights, may wish to purchase a photoplay for distribution which has already been completed by a third party. There is no standard deal made in acquiring a film. It is simply a matter of bargaining. The various types of deals that are made were discussed earlier in connection with production-distribution agreements and deals with independent distributors.

There is no rule of thumb for the term of the license of a photoplay. The distributor will ordinarily figure a theatrical release followed by the possibility of either network television or television syndication, and the new uses coming in, such as cartridge television and pay television, as well as community antenna television, which means that a photoplay can have a good deal of residual value over a protracted period of time. Most purchasers acquire rights for at least ten or fifteen years, and all of them will try to get rights in perpetuity if possible. Certain procedures should always be followed to determine the producer's rights in the photoplay.

Ordinarily, a producer who wants to acquire distribution rights in a photoplay produced outside of the U.S. will take a number of preliminary steps. First, he should check the U.S. Copyright Office to make sure that the photoplay has not been copyrighted here by somebody else. Second, if the production company which is licensing the photoplay for distribution is a U.S. corporation, a check should be made for tax liens or financing statements listing the production company as debtor, for it is possible that the photoplay being sold has already been mortgaged. As discussed, many photoplays produced outside of the U.S. are produced under co-production agreements in order to secure the advantages of aid from more than one country.

In both France and Italy there is a central film registry equivalent to our copyright office registration. All documents affecting the production of the motion picture photoplay are supposed to be recorded in this registry, and if these documents are not recorded, a subsequent assignee recording may prevail against a prior assignee which does not record. Therefore, the producer should request the company licensing the rights to him to furnish him with a certified copy of extracts from the motion picture film registry so that he may know exactly what rights are outstanding. In the typical French-Italian co-production, rights are usually held by banks lending money to the production, subdistributors who have acquired distribution rights in certain territories in return for advances, and sometimes by talent who have profit participations and deferments.

The purchaser should also examine the agreement pursuant to which the underlying rights in the literary property were acquired, the screenwriter's agreement, the director's agreement, and the principal cast members' agreements. In most foreign countries, matters covered by contract in the U.S. are covered by statute in the foreign countries so that the foreign contracts will be incomplete. This is where the typical trouble spot is found in preparing foreign agreements.

In addition, remember that in most European countries there is the well-established tradition of *droit moral*, or moral rights. Under this theory, there are certain inalienable rights of the author of an artistic work which he cannot contract away. Note, however, that under the moral rights statutes and regardless of a

178

contract, the director has the right to prevent cutting and editing of his film for any reason. In addition, there may even be a question of the artistic license of the director to change the underlying work, other than to make it suitable for the medium in which the director is working, if the photoplay is based on an underlying work. There seems to be some generally accepted custom that a photoplay, in spite of the concept of *droit moral,* can be cut and edited for television exhibition or for legal censorship. Again, the case law on the subject is very sketchy even in the courts in which *droit moral* applies.

There is further difficulty in that under some foreign jurisdictions an author cannot create a work as an employee and can only convey rights in a literary property for a certain stated period of years. This must be considered in granting distribution rights. There are also in some countries certain statutes that will entitle an author to a certain percentage of any resale or any relicensing of rights. Ordinarily, producers in foreign jurisdictions will take care of these problems in their contracts with the authors, but the statutes and contracts should be checked. The foreign producer circumvents the law in some cases by giving the authors his compensation as an advance against a miniscule percentage of net profits, which assures that no net profits above the advance will ever be payable.

An additional difficulty with foreign-made motion pictures results from the complexity of the billing clauses. Quite frequently, even more so than in the U.S., producers trade billing credit for money. In other words, rather than pay the talent large sums of money, they will promise the talent good billing credit. This may make it very difficult to set up an effective ad. In addition, different artists may get different billings in different countries. For instance, if there is an important Italian artist and an important French artist, the Italian artist may be billed in first position in Italy, and the French artist may be billed in first position in France.

To the extent that there are any liens or security interests in the film, or to the extent that any of the talent have bona fide net profit participations or deferments, it is usually wise to get a *non-disturbance letter* from such persons. The letter will acknowledge that the producer has the right to enter into the agreement with the purchaser, and that the person executing the non-disturbance letter will not interfere with the purchaser's rights and will look only to the producer in connection with the enforcement of his rights. This is upheld no matter how the producer breaches his agreement with the purchaser, so long as the purchaser performs under the distribution agreement. If these non-disturbance letters are secured, even if the producer is in default, it is quite certain that a creditor or a dissatisfied artist would not be able to interfere with the purchaser's rights.

In addition to the non-disturbance letters, the distributor (purchaser) will do well to transfer the copyright of the motion picture to his name for his territory. This way, the distributor will be the copyright proprietor and legal owner of the photoplay, and this will put him in a better legal position vis-a-vis his licensor if there are disputes. The purchaser will also get the benefit of the investment tax credit permitting accelerated depreciation for which copyright ownership is a prerequisite. In the event the licensor insists upon being the copyright proprietor of the photoplay, and to the extent that the distributor is giving a cash advance or minimum guarantee or incurring expenses for prints and advertising, the purchaser should have a security interest in the photoplay for the distribution territory to secure the rights. Financing statements and a mortgage of copyright in the U.S. Copyright Office should be filed in the proper places to perfect that security interest. The purchaser should have also a laboratory pledge-holder's agreement from the laboratory where preprint materials are stored, assuring that the distributor's orders will at all times be honored.

Chapter Fifteen

DISTRIBUTION AGREEMENTS FOR A COMPLETED FILM

In the earlier chapters, problems involving the concept of gross receipts and net receipts, the negotiation of a P-D pursuant to which a distributor finances the cost of production of a film, and certain alternate methods of financing the production of a film were discussed. Assuming the film has been self-financed and is now ready for distribution, the two potential sources of theatrical distribution in the U.S. are through the "majors" and through the smaller independent film distributors, the "independents." The difference in the two entities is that the smaller independent film distributor does not maintain its own distribution facilities throughout the entire U.S. Usually, the smaller independent will itself distribute in the area around it or its home base, i.e. New York or Los Angeles. In other parts of the country independents will distribute through self-distributors who are called states righters.

States righters operate in certain states or territories of the U.S. in which they arrange for booking the picture in theatres in those areas. The usual deal between the independent and the states righters is for the independent to finance the cost of prints and advertising and for the states righters to distribute for a distribution fee of 25% of the gross receipts of the film after deducting cooperative advertising costs. The independent distributor keeps close control over the activities of the states righters and retains certain rights to determine the method of release in the states righters' territory, the particular theatre in which the film is exhibited and even the terms of the exhibition deals with the theatres. The producer negotiating the terms of a deal with an independent will determine whether the independent's gross receipts are the states righters' gross receipts (in which event the independent is a guarantor of collection), or the independent's gross receipts are merely those sums actually received from the states righters. In the former case, gross receipts would be defined as whatever the independent or any subdistributor of the film receives from the theatres. The independent then either runs the risk of assuming that the states righters will in fact report all to the independent or allowing that the producer be paid out of only what the independent receives. Another question the producer must settle with an independent is whether or not the independent's distribution fee is tacked on to the states righters' distribution fee or absorbed into the states righters' distribution fee.

There is no rule of thumb for the kind of deal that can be made with a distributor for a completed film. This is solely a matter of bargaining, and the producer's bargaining position depends upon the quality of the film and how many people are interested in distributing it. Many of the principles discussed in connection with the negotiating of the P-D also come into play here. Some of them will be enumerated.

1. Cash advance or guarantee—obviously if a producer can receive a cash advance or guarantee equal to or exceeding his cost of production, he has the advantage of insuring his investors that they will be repaid for their capital contributions and be protected against loss. This will encourage his investors to invest in other projects. The disadvantage of receiving a cash advance or minimum guarantee is that the division of gross receipts between the distributor and the producer will be much less favorable to the producer. This is because the distributor, by paying a substantial advance or

182

guarantee, has in essence financed the cost of production of the film.

2. If there is not going to be any substantial cash advance or minimum guarantee, the producer's negotiating tactic is to share immediately in the gross receipts of the film. Under the P-D form of agreement, the distributor first deducts distribution fees, then distribution expenses, and then recoups the cost of production. If the distributor tried to make a similar deal with a producer coming to the distributor with a completed film. the distributor would first recoup its distribution fees and distribution expenses and pay the balance to the producer. The balance would then be used by the producer to recoup production costs and whatever is remaining would be profits. The producer's difficulty with this is that the distributor is recouping its investment (fees and expenses) prior to the producer. The advantages to a producer, if the film is a substantial success, are that the producer will be able to recoup the cost of production and will receive the balance of the income as profits.

Because producers are not usually willing to wait for the return of their investment, they negotiate for a division of gross receipts. Under an old formula, the distributor kept 70% of the gross receipts (to cover the distributor's distribution fee and prints and advertising) and the producer received 30% of the gross receipts (toward recoupment of the cost of production and profits). Most usually now the distributor receives 65% and the producer 35%. Sometimes the percentages change after a specified dollar volume of gross receipts. For example, the agreement may provide that the distributor receive 70% of the first million, 60% of the second million, and 50% of everything over the second million. The theory of the sliding percentage is that the bulk of the distributor's print and advertising costs would be incurred in the first million of gross receipts, and those costs would be reduced in the second and third million.

Another possibility is to let the distributor first recoup a smaller distribution fee (only to cover overhead) and then provide that the balance of the gross receipts be divided in proportion to the distributor's investment in prints and advertising and the producer's investment in the cost of production, with any profits divided in the same manner. It is possible to make one arrangement for theatrical distribution and another arrangement for television and non-theatrical distribution

3. In dealing with independent distributors or distributors without television sales facilities, it is possible to negotiate a deal whereby the producer retains television and non-theatrical rights. The producer would agree not to exercise those rights for a stated period of time to protect the theatrical release. The producer dealing with an independent would also probably have a better chance to retain music publishing rights and rights in new media. Again, however, this is a matter of bargaining.

4. In connection with sales policies of an independent distributor a producer has a better chance of negotiating either on a maximum or minimum for advertising (depending on the deal), an obligation on the part of the distributor to release the film in certain key cities within a certain period of time, to open the film in a certain theatre or a specified group of theatres in New York, Los Angeles or some other key city, and to spend a specified amount in connection with that opening. Some producers will engage a producer's representative who will have the right to approve certain exhibition agreements and will consult generally about sales policies involved in the distribution of the film. In addition, some producers may be able to insist that their own advertising campaign be utilized.

5. Although under the P-D, rights are ordinarily granted in perpetuity, it may be possible to establish a shorter distribution period for the independent distributor. At the end of the shorter period, the rights would revert to the producer.

6. Because of the potential instability of some of the smaller independents, the producer can negotiate for security documentation to secure payment of the producer's share of gross receipts. In addition, the producer can ask that his money be segregated and deposited in a special trust account in his name.

184

There is obviously no pattern for the various types of negotiations that can be carried out. Some of the independents are in a position to give a picture personalized service and cooperate intensively with the producer in the distribution of the film. Usually, the smaller independent is a one or two-man company and that one person will himself arrange for the key city exhibition agreements, prepare the advertising campaign, and guide the distribution of the film. If the person in the distribution company is capable, the producer will have obvious advantages. On the other hand, many of the smaller independents have only been in the business for a few years and their financial structure may be unstable.

All of the arrangements just discussed apply only to the U.S. A producer has the option of conveying rights throughout the world to a major distributor with a distribution facilities in foreign countries; however, the distributor may want to cross-collateralize receipts in the foreign territories, so that losses in one territory will offset profits in another. There is also the possibility of the producer making his own distribution deals on a territory-by-territory distribution overseas. The producer can arrange for this distribution himself by having the film exhibited in the various foreign film festivals and possibly submitting the film for awards, or by employing agents who specialize in procuring foreign distribution deals. The advantages of a territory-by-territory arrangement is a more precise structuring of each deal to a particular territory involved. The disadvantage is the necessity of dealing with a number of distributors and the difficulty of checking distribution statements and collecting the money due.

Chapter Sixteen

THEATRICAL EXHIBITION AGREEMENTS WITH EXHIBITOR

After the producer has made his deal for distribution of a photoplay, or completed the production of a film, how is the photoplay released by the distributor to the theatres in the U.S.? Let us first examine a theatre exhibition agreement between a distributor and an exhibitor.

Almost all exhibition agreements contain standard boilerplate provisions which exhibitors have never negotiated. Distributors claim that these clauses are an integral part of the contract and enforceable by their terms. Exhibitors commonly say that the boilerplate means nothing at all, and the terms and conditions of the agreement are really governed by trade practices within the industry. Ordinarily, exhibitors execute exhibition agreements without change. In the event the distributor wants to vary the usual form of exhibition agreement in any material respect, the change is thoroughly publicized and discussed with the exhibitor, either generally or through the exhibitor's trade associations. Quite frequently, the exhibition agreements are either not executed at all, or are incomplete in one or more respects. Since so many deals are made, some branch personnel never bother getting

187

signatures and some contracts are executed not by the exhibitors, but by a booking agent on behalf of an exhibitor.

However, for example, assume an exhibition agreement has been properly completed and executed. The agreement will commonly list the name of the theatre, the corporate name of the exhibitor, and the town and state. It will also list the title of the picture, and the extent of the engagement (that is, whether for one week, two weeks, or more). Pictures are licensed in a number of ways: either on the basis of the division of gross box office receipts, or for a flat sum, or on the basis of a division of box office receipts after the exhibitor has recouped a house expense (the cost of the operation of the theatre). In any case of a division of box office receipts, there may or may not be a minimum guaranteed film rental paid by the exhibitor to the distributor.

Ordinarily, the *house expense figure* is a figure which includes a profit margin over and above the actual direct out-of-pocket expense of operating the theatre. Sometimes, the house expense figure is audited by a distributor and a fair amount of bargaining can go on so as to establish the house figure. Once the figure is established, however, all distributors generally continue to utilize the figure unless the exhibitor wishes to increase the figure because of increased operating expenses.

Occasionally, the division of box office receipts is based on a sliding scale. In other words, the distributor receives an increasing percentage of box office receipts, depending on the amount of the gross receipts. The higher the gross, the higher the distributor's share of box office receipts. If an exhibition contract has a percentage in it reading "25-50," this means that the distributor receives a minimum of 25% of the box office receipts and that percentage escalates until a ceiling of 50% is reached. The distributor and exhibitor work out dollar amounts for each percentage. For instance, 25% may equal $10,000, 26% may equal $11,000, 27% may equal $12,000, and so on.

The theory is that the 25% figure (or whatever the lowest percentage is) is supposed to equal the theatre's operating expense. In other words, if the gross box office receipts for a particular week do not exceed the 25% figure, the exhibitor keeps all of the receipts and the distributor does not get anything.

Some of the more important pictures play on the basis of a

188

90-10 division over the house floor. In other words, the exhibitor and distributor agree to a figure which presumably covers the exhibitor's overhead. Actually, this figure leaves a profit margin for the exhibitor. Any gross box office receipts in excess of that figure are divided 90% to the distributor and 10% to the exhibitor. The advantage of this agreement to the distributor is that if the theatre has large grossing potential and the picture is an extremely popular one, the distributor can make more money than if the distributor were receiving merely 50% or 60% of the box office receipts. On the other hand, if the picture is unsuccessful, the distributor may end up losing money because he is almost always responsible for the entire cooperative advertising costs. Sometimes the agreement can even call for a 90-10 division over the house expense, but in no event less than 50% or 60% of the gross box office receipts. Exhibitors will agree to this type of provision only for highly successful pictures.

Recently, some distributors have either leased theatres and operated them themselves, or licensed theatres from the exhibitor-owners. In the lease concept, the distributor takes over the theatre and runs it—that is, the distributor hires the management and pays the employees and acts as a regular lessee would act. Under a license arrangement, the distributor pays a weekly sum to the theatre owner to cover the threatre owner's overhead plus an agreed upon profit. The theatre owner, from that sum, pays the theatre overhead and continues to engage and pay the help, etc., but the distributor has the right to decide what pictures will play in the theatre for what period of time and on what terms. The distributor is booking the theatre and to that extent, acting like an exhibitor. If the distributor is successful, he may make a profit. If not, he stands to take a loss, but, in any event, the exhibitor has a guaranteed profit. The advantage of either the lease or the license arrangement to a distributor is that the theatre is always available to play pictures distributed by the distributor, and therefore, there will always be an outlet for the distributor's product.

Another arrangement for licensing films is to license them on a flat sale basis. In other words, the exhibitor will pay a fixed sum for the engagement. The exhibitor keeps all of the box office receipts and ordinarily pays for all of the advertising.

All of the methods of contractual dealing between exhibitors and distributors are subject to the peculiar patterns of distribution of motion pictures and these patterns are very closely governed by concepts of anti-trust. Let us examine this in some detail.

The underlying concept of motion picture distribution is that the distribution is conducted in waves. Ordinarily, a picture will open in one or two theatres, then be released in a first neighborhood run, and then go to second and subsequent runs. The reason for this is that no distributor can manufacture enough prints of the picture to play every theatre at the same time. Therefore, if a picture opens in key cities around the country in one or two theatres in each city, then plays selected neighborhood engagements, and is saturated in one market at a time, a distributor can get by with a fewer number of prints than would be the case if he were obligated to play all of the theatres simultaneously. In determining whether or not to take a particular engagement or to enter into a licensing agreement with the theatre, the distributor has got to make sure that there are prints available to service the engagements. One of the prime functions of the distributor's print department is keeping track of where the prints are, and which prints will be available on what dates, so that the sales department does not book too many theatres. If more prints are ordered than are absolutely necessary, additional distribution expenses are being incurred and for no reason .

There are some terms commonly used in connection with the exhibition of motion pictures and the licensing arrangements between the distributor and the exhibitor. A *run* is a period of time during which a theatre plays a picture. In the licensing agreement, it may be stipulated that the theatre must play a particular picture for a given number of weeks. A *holdover* is the right of a distributor or exhibitor to insist that the theatre be obligated to exhibit the picture in the theatre for additional weeks under certain circumstances. Usually, the circumstance is that box office receipts must equal a contracted minimum weekly figure. *Clearance* is the fixed amount of time one theatre will limit use of the film in another theatre. For instance, if a license agreement is entered into with theatre A and it is given a run for a particular date, it will want to make sure that the picture will not be exhibited in theatre B (a competitive theatre) at the same time. Consequently, he makes a condition of the exhibition agreement the fact that the picture

190

will not play in theatre B until a certain fixed period of time after the conclusion of the engagement at A's theatre.

The *availability* is the date a distributor makes a given motion picture available to an exhibitor. Generally, the distributor has the right to set any availability date that it wishes to set. The anti-trust problems generally arise because of difference of opinions between distributors and exhibitors or, possibly, exhibitors with each other, as to which theatres are competitive with each other.

Ordinarily each distributor makes a determination initially as to which theatres are competitive with each other. This is ordinarily done by periodic surveys. A sales representative of the distributor will visit the theatres and make a judgment as to the distance one theatre is from another, the population from which each draws it patrons, parking facilities, the ease of or availability of public transportation between one theatre and another, and seating capacities, among other things. After this determination has been made, the distributor will negotiate with each one of the theatres in the zone for a particular run. If one of the theatres believes that it is not getting a fair opportunity to acquire a product, that theatre can request competitive bidding, and if the theatre is within the competitive zone, the distributor ordinarily will allow all of the theatres in that zone to bid for the picture for that run on the availability date.

The bidding procedure is quite simple. The distributor will send all of the theatre owners a notice setting forth the number of theatres within the particular zone that the distributor wishes to license, the availability date, and any minimum terms the distributor wishes to impose. Most distributors wish to make the bid as vague as possible so as to give themselves flexibility in determining which bid to accept. The bids can either offer a cash advance against the distributor's share of box office receipts, or whatever other terms the exhibitor wishes to bid in order to get the picture. The offer generally provides that bids must be returned by a specified date and if any bids are received after that date, they will not be accepted. After all of the bids have been received, the distributor opens the bids and decides which, if any, he wants to accept. The exercise of the distributor's discretion on which bids to accept and which to reject has sometimes led to litigation, but, in theory, the distributor is entitled to accept any bid in the

191

exercise of reasonable business judgment.

If one theatre has demonstrated a superior grossing capacity, that theatre will ordinarily get the picture unless a smaller theatre, which has shown less grossing capacity, is willing to pay a substantial cash advance or agree to some other provisions that make the engagement at the smaller theatre more attractive. The distributor can decide to reject all of the bids, in which event it then can negotiate separately with each theatre in order to make a deal.

Although the concept of competitive bidding is attractive from the distributor's point of view, it is not from the exhibitor's point of view. In the ordinary exhibition agreement between the distributor and an exhibitor, there is an implied or even an express understanding that if the picture is not satisfactory, the exhibitor will be able to get some relief from the contractual terms.

The renegotiation that follows an unsuccessful engagement is called an *adjustment*. The amount of the adjustment or whether or not there will be an adjustment is solely dependent upon bargaining. If the distributor refuses to make the adjustment, there is always the risk that the exhibitor will refuse to play the distributor's product, or will not agree to the same contractual terms in the future for other pictures. However, in a bidding situation, there can be no adjustments, because any adjustment would give rise to the claim that the bidding was rigged and that the successful bidder had a side deal whereby some of the terms would later be reduced or relaxed. For this reason, exhibitors do not want to bid against each other.

One way to avoid bidding is to claim that one theatre is not competitive with another theatre. A theatre owner may claim that rather than bidding against another theatre, he should be entitled to play *day and date* with that theatre. This means that two theatres play the same picture commencing at the same time. It is conceivable that two theatres may not, strictly speaking, be competitive with each other, but that bidding is instituted because the distributor has only a limited number of prints for the particular run.

For instance, if a distributor wants to play a picture in a city that has only one print available, and only wants to open the picture in one theatre in that city, the competitive bid for that city might conceivably include all of the first run theatres in that city. Two theatres, each one on the opposite side of town, could argue that they were not competitive with each other, and that both should have the right to play the picture. That might be true, but if the distributor has right to select the number of prints that will be made available for a particular engagement, how can it judge which of the two theatres should play the picture except by bidding the theatres? One theatre can argue that he should not be forced to bid against the other theatre and that the distributor and the other theatre are conspiring together in violation of the anti-trust laws to drive him out of business. This is the stuff of which motion picture exhibition lawsuits are made.

In addition to questions concerning the theatres which bid against each other, a different distinction can be made in figuring the theatres that will be competitively bidding based on the distributor's assessment of the theatre's grossing power. If the theatre is a smaller theatre, not as well maintained as a larger one, it may automatically be relegated to a subsequent run and not be invited to engage in competitive bidding at all. Contrariwise, a theatre which is offered competitive bidding for a first run may decide to accept competitive bidding for a second or third run.

As already stated, most of the film distribution today takes place in a pattern of waves emanating from a big city. Ordinarily, one or two theatres in the heart of the city play the picture first; then on a subsequent run, showcase neighborhood theatres play the picture, and finally, the local neighborhood theatres play the picture.

One question which has plagued the film industry is what happens when there are two cities fairly close to each other and one city starts playing the picture before the other city. Imagine, for instance, a situation in which one city is 50 miles north of another one and there are theatres located directly in between the two cities. If city A plays the picture before city B, the theatres which are considered to be in the zone encompassing city A will be playing the picture earlier than the theatres considered to be in the zone encompassing city B, even though the theatres in A and those theatres in B on the periphery of the zones may be very close to each other. In that case, should the zones be modified so as to include some theatres not originally in the zone, or should the zones remain the way they are? The zones are usually set up based upon historical factors, but as populations shift and new theatres are built, the zones may be subject to change. Contributing to the problem is the fact that some theatre owners deliberately build their theatres in such a way as to fit within the zone most beneficial to them, while at the same time drawing on the patronage and the population of the other zone.

When a theatre is built right on the border, the theatre owner will insist that he be part of zone A as opposed to zone B. This poses a problem for the distributors. If the distributors agree, the other theatre owners located at the periphery of zone B, and very near this new theatre, which is now in zone A, will claim that they are competitive with that theatre and should bid against it. If, on the other hand, the new theatre is placed in zone B, that theatre owner (like the other zone B periphery theatres) will claim that he is competitive with the periphery theatres in zone A and should bid against those theatres and not play subsequent to them. Again, there is no answer to this kind of question, and each case turns on its own facts. Unfortunately, the costs of anti-trust litigation in the distribution field are substantial and add to the woes of the distributor.

In addition to this, there are other problems. In some cities, distributors claim that theatre owners have gotten together and have divided up the available product. This is called a *split of product*. One theatre owner will only play the pictures of certain distributors and the other theatre owners will play the pictures of the balance of the distributors. This pattern tends to defeat competitive bidding.

Exhibitors resent the fact that they are sometimes forced to engage in what is known as *blind bidding*. This happens when a distributor has a picture but for various reasons cannot or will not show it to the exhibitors prior to the time at which the exhibitors are asked to bid for the picture. The exhibitors claim that blind bidding defeats competitive bidding. Some distributors must blind bid because the picture is not ready for release enough in advance to have exhibition screening. This will give the exhibitor the right to terminate the agreement prior to the exhibition of the picture if after the exhibitor has seen the picture, the exhibitor decides not to play it. However, some of the smaller exhibitors feel that the large chains of theatres sometimes use their circuit buying power

194

to coerce distributors into giving them preferential treatment.

The advertising of each particular theatre engagement is carried out by agreement between distributors and exhibitors. The press book, which contains sample advertising, is given to the exhibitor along with whatever publicity and promotional materials are available, and the exhibitor and distributor enter into a *cooperative advertising agreement* for the particular engagement, indicating the amount of money to be spent on advertising and where the advertising will be placed. Ordinarily, the exhibitor will have the right to select the particular newspaper or radio station in the market in which advertising will be placed, and the exhibitor will also select from the press book the type of advertising that the exhibitor wants. Sometimes the exhibitor will prepare his own advertising, even though this is a violation of the exhibition contract with the distributor. The distributor and the exhibitor share the advertising costs as part of the negotiated agreement and usually the costs are shared in proportion to the division of box office receipts. On the 90-10 deal over the house floor, the distributor ordinarily pays for all of the advertising.

As an example of how the exhibition of a film may be conducted, each distributor has a series of sales offices in the major cities in the U.S. The major motion picture distributors used to have as many as 30 of these offices but this number has been cut down in recent years, and, now most of the distributors have somewhere between 10 and 20. These offices are called *film exchanges*. The word "exchange" means the exchange of a print from one theatre to another. The exchange usually comprises one or more salesmen, bookkeepers, and, secretaries. The salesmen report to the general sales manager or possibly to a division head who is responsible for a number of exchanges. Each exchange not only serves a particular city, but a whole geographical area. Each salesman will have a detailed knowledge of each theatre in the exchange area and will be able to tell you the location of the theatre, the grossing capacity, what the theatre is playing, how well the picture is doing, what the theatre will be playing next, how many seats the theatre holds, etc.

The general sales manager, or the division manager, will instruct the salesmen in the exchange in the general distribution policies with respect to a particular theatre, and the kind of terms that the distributor wishes for the particular picture. The division manager may also tell the salesmen the preferred theatres for the particular picture and whom to call on. If the particular engagement is a bidding engagement, the head of the exchange will prepare and send out the bid forms and receive the bids. These are, depending on the particular factors of the distributor, handled at the local level or forwarded to the main offices of the organization. Most of the major decisions are made either by the general sales manager or the division manager, and a large part of the exchange function is to call on the various distributors, tell them what is available, and find out what deals can be made. The major deals are usually made by the head of the exchange or by the general sales manager.

When an agreement has been reached between the distributor and the exhibitor with respect to a particular picture, the exchange sends out the distributor's printed form of agreement. The exchange also will fill in whatever information must be filled in the agreement setting forth the terms, the run, any clearance, etc.

When the exhibitor signs the contract, the contract is forwarded to New York or accepted in New York. This is done for a number of reasons. First, it helps to eliminate the concept that a distributor is doing business in various states where it does not have an exchange, but where salesmen travel soliciting engagements for pictures. Second, it gives the general sales manager in the New York office a chance to review all of the contracts and make sure they are in order. The sales manager countersigns the contract and sends one copy back to the exchange for forwarding to the exhibitor, sends another copy to the exchange and the remaining copies to various departments in the distribution organization.

About a week or two prior to the engagement, the parties will agree with respect to the cooperative engagement, and the cooperative advertising agreement will be entered into, itemizing the advertising. The exchange will arrange for the print to be delivered to the theatre and for the print to be picked up at the end of the engagement. If you multiply this function by a picture which can have 5,000 or more exhibitions during its theatrical release, you can understand the complexity of the distribution business.

Chapter Seventeen

CONCLUSION

Putting a film together is an extremely complex process. It is hoped that the reader will at least gain from this book an awareness of the interdependence of all the parts necessary to form the totality which becomes the film. The reader should also have learned that in this industry, the unexpected is to be anticipated.

But could you predict, for example, that a producer negotiating a production-distribution agreement might be frustrated in wrapping up the deal because the director, who is part of the package, is making different demands which affect the financier's deal with the producer? The producer has done his job well, has acquired the motion picture rights to a best-selling novel, and has interested one of the most important directors in making the movie. But the negotiations drag on and seem incapable of resolution. The director is making less reasonable demands (since his bargaining power is greater) and the producer cannot consummate the deal with the distributor-financier until the director makes his deal. Both the producer and director are on the same team, so to speak, but the producer wants the deal more and faster than the director, and yet his deal is totally dependent on the director's negotiations also being favorably concluded.

What so often happens in this business is that the parties agree in principle to an arrangement which must then be reduced to writing. The lawyers then attempt to make the contract, which of necessity must be much more thorough and contain many items not originally discussed or even contemplated. So the lawyers are faulted for their thoroughness (admittedly, sometimes they should be faulted for their unbelievable "nit-picking," their dedication to meaningless minutae, sometimes mislabeled as "thoroughness"), and the negotiations become bogged down. The lawyers' fault, of course.

Lawyers don't make deals—they prepare the contracts of their clients which set forth the deals made by the parties. Of course, this is enough of an oversimplification to be almost untrue. Constructive lawyers can help make deals and unimaginative lawyers can mess up deals. But at the same time, some of the deals initially made are not deals at all, and when the parties examine all of the undecided issues, they find that they have more disagreement than agreement. Thank the lawyer for preventing the marriage (which is easier) which would likely end in divorce (which could be costly and catastrophic).

The most important thing that one must learn in negotiating and making a film is where, if one must, to acquiesce in a compromise. There are some artistic compromises that would destroy the value of a film, and there are also some business compromises that would make the venture foolhardy. What is most important is knowing what is important. This one learns by acquiring knowledge, by intuiting, and by doing.

Hopefully, this book will have contributed to the "acquiring of knowledge." The "intuiting," if you are lucky, you will have been born with. The "doing," of course, you must experience yourself by doing.

In the introduction it was noted that this book was not easy to write and will not be easy to read. It must now be added that writing it was a meaningful experience and, hopefully reading it will have been a meaningful experience for you.